Mario Andretti, auto-racing daredevil, conquered the Indianapolis 500 with his face still blistered from burns suffered in a spectacular and nearly fatal crash of a few weeks earlier. He earned over $500,000, racing in 1969. A quiet family man, father of three children, Andretti is a perfect union of powerful muscles, nerves of steel and a fierce drive to win. This is the complete story of his rise from a poverty-stricken childhood in Italy to winning the richest and most coveted prize in auto racing.

——————————

This Tempo Books *edition contains the complete text of the original hard-cover edition.*

ANDRETTI

BY BILL LIBBY

TEMPO
BOOKS

GROSSET & DUNLAP
A NATIONAL GENERAL COMPANY
Publishers   *New York*

Contents

Acknowledgments

The author wishes to thank Mario Andretti and his wife, Dee Ann, Clint Brawner, Jim McGee, Andy Granatelli, and the late Al Dean for their time and talk over the years. He wishes also to thank for their help in one way or another Donald Davidson and Dick Jordan of USAC; Al Bloemker, Charlene Ellis, and Bud Jones of the Indianapolis Motor Speedway; Bob Shafer and Bob Thomas of Ontario Motor Speedway; Chuck Barnes, Jr., and Bill Marvel, Jr., of Sports Headliners, Inc.; Lyle Kenyon Engel, Dennis Bender, John Meador, William Dredge, Allan Krause, John Fowler, Paul Preuss, and others at *Sport* and *Car Life* Magazines and Motorbooks, Inc.; and Ford, Firestone, and STP companies. The author especially wishes to express gratitude to Bob Tronolone for providing many of the photographs in this book and to the other photographers represented.

For JACK ZANGER, STEVE GELMAN and AL SILVERMAN, foremost among those in the field who have been friends and who have helped above and beyond any call of duty.

1. The Professional

MARIO ANDRETTI is a professional race driver. It is his pleasure and his passion and it consumes his life. He sits on a pit wall fooling with the visor on his crash helmet. He is wearing immaculate flame-proof white coveralls. His black hair is neatly combed. His hands and his fingernails are clean. He shows us a pair of soft leather gloves, like golfer's gloves, which he uses to grip the steering wheel of his racing car. "They're made special for me," he points out. With him, everything has to be just right.

He is a little dandy, small and neat and handsome. He is only five feet, six inches and weighs 135 pounds, but he is wiry and strong and tough, and size is of no great advantage to a race driver, anyway. He is twenty-nine years old and looks no older, but seems older. He is a sports hero, but he is quiet and reserved. He hides his eyes and the thoughts they may reveal behind extravagant sunglasses. Fans, writers, officials and other drivers come up to chat with him or simply to stand near him and watch him and he is polite to all of them, but you know that he does not give much of himself to anyone. He is proud rather than vain, but he enjoys his celebrity. "I eat this stuff up," he says.

His mechanics are operating in the guts of his car. Its belly laid open, it is an ominous red monster, gleaming with thirty coats of wax and the decals of thirty automotive firms on its flanks. It is a wedge-shaped, rear-engined car, twelve feet long, three feet wide, three feet high, weighing only 1,250 pounds. Its engine juts from the rear, silent for the moment. On the track, similar cars whine and roar and belch smoke, and the nasty smell of burning fuel fills the air as they proceed through practice routines, roaring around at speeds of greater than 150 miles per hour, speeds which stagger a normal man's imagination.

"I love racing," he says. "It's all I ever wanted to do as long as I can remember. I love best being good at it. If I wasn't good at it, I wouldn't want to bother with it. I'd rather do something else." He is good at it. In his first two years on the U. S. championship circuit, the major leagues of American auto racing, he won the national driving title. The next two years he was a close second. "Second is no good," he says. "Third is no good. The only thing that's any good is first place. When I lose, I feel like cutting my throat. I love racing, but only when I win."

He was born and reared in Italy and still speaks with traces of an Italian accent, but he matured in his profession in the United States. He has been driving race cars since he was thirteen, but so has his twin brother, Aldo, and while Mario has reached the heights, Aldo has crashed and struggled and despaired. They are similar and started out together, all even, but one has made it while the other has not. Auto-racing is the cruellest sport and not an easy one to conquer. Men are killed or crippled from racing crashes every year.

Mario is married and a family man, but he is unafraid. "I'm no fool," he says. "I know something could happen. It's always there. The risks are what make it special. I wouldn't want to do what thirty thousand other men could." It is pointed out that he has been fortunate so far in his career, having had few major accidents and never having been seriously hurt. What a thing to mention! He shakes his head and makes a face of wistful bitterness. "They say you don't know how good you are until you've had a bad one," he says. "They say then you'll find out how you come back from one. All the other stuff doesn't mean anything until you show you can come back from one. We'll see," he says.

He is a rich young man, earning more than a quarter of a million dollars from racing triumphs and endorsements every year. No other athletes have the opportunity to make the money a top racing driver can make. No other athletes are sponsored by so many firms with as much money to spend on advertising as race drivers, who are backed by car manufacturers and tire firms and gasoline companies. "It's not the money," he shrugs. "If no one was paying anything, I'd do this for nothing. Since they're paying, I want a piece of the pie. But it's not the money." Nor, he says, is it the glory, not any more, anyway. "I've had that," he says. "It's the winning."

He has won everything except the Indianapolis 500. This is 1969 and he has yet to win the Indianapolis 500. He has won many championship races and the national title and he has won the Daytona 500 stock car classic and the Sebring twelve-hour sports car classic, but he has not yet won Indy. He has not even come close.

He has won the pole position as the fastest qualifier two years in a row, but he has not come close to winning the race. His first year he finished third, but it was not a close third, and his last two years he has broken down early and finished far back. Last year he finished last, which was humiliating to a proud person.

The Indianapolis 500 is the world's single most spectacular annual sporting event. Every May it draws a million persons and in recent Mays has been approaching payoffs of a million dollars. On race day, Memorial Day, a crowd of more than 300,000 persons packs into the sprawling arena, and the drivers risk their lives for a first-place purse of more than $200,000. It is not just the money. It is the glory. And the winning. "It's not right that this race should be worth all the others, but it is," Mario says, complaining coolly. "I've won everything else, but I know it's like I was nothing until I win this. So this is what I want to win. Not the others. This one."

This is Indianapolis, May, 1969, three days before the beginning of qualifying time trials and ten days before the race. Mario is ready to practice now. His red car is buttoned up. He stands looking at it. How does he feel? How did he sleep last night? He feels fine, he says. He never has any trouble sleeping, he says. "This stuff doesn't bother me," he says. "I don't sweat." Not even being crowded at these moments? "There's always people around," he says. "When I get in the car, I'm alone."

He goes to his car, which does not even rise crotch-high. He ties a bandana around his mouth and pulls on his helmet and crawls into the low-slung racer, until he is not so much sitting as he is lying on his back in the cramped, padded cockpit. He can barely see over the hood. He is flanked by fuel tanks and by the wide tires, which are higher than his head. He straps on his seat belt and shoulder harness, lowers a sun visor over his eyes and buckles his helmet strap. He pulls on his gloves and lays his hands on the wheel. His face seems expressionless as his crew leans over him and talks to him about his run.

The point of a starter is plunged into the rear of the racer as Mario punches a button and the engine roars to resounding life with flashes of gray flame. Smoothly, he steers out onto the paved track, and begins to circle the two-and-one-half-mile oval slowly at first, then faster and faster. Soon he is screaming down the straights at more than 225 miles per hour and averaging around 170 miles per hour for each tour, while observers, awed by his prominence, admire his style.

Then the rear end of his car collapses and the right rear wheel tears off and the car lurches into a skid as onlookers shout and scream. The car smashes into a concrete wall with horrible force and a shriek of rending metal and a flash of fire and comes spinning off the wall and across the track, coming apart in pieces, large pieces, a third of the car here and a quarter there, debris raining through the air like shrapnel after a bomb has exploded on a battlefield, until like some torn and broken creature it settles in its various pieces and is still, except for the smoke rising from the wreckage and the fire burning the main portion, in which Andretti seems trapped.

Even as Andy Granatelli, the sponsor, fat and puffing, runs for him, knowing, as everyone there knows that no man can survive such a flaming, smashing hell, Andretti is scrambling from it, and walking from it, counting his limbs and holding his hands to his burned face, hurting, cursing the fates and thanking God for survival all at once under his breath, while others are shouting at him and running to him.

2. The Toy Tiger

*SPEAKING of auto-racing, Mario An-
dretti says, "Right from the beginning I
loved it so much. I know there's men making a living at it, a good living at it, and I
am going to do it. I don't care if I work
twenty-four hours a day at it. Every
morning when I get up, it's the first thing
I think about."*

Mario Andretti was born February 28, 1940,
five hours ahead of twin brother Aldo, in Mon-

tana, Italy, on the Istrian peninsula near Yugoslavia. They also had a sister, Anna Maria.

This was wartime. Mario recalls, "I grew up with war. I remember American soldiers around near the end of the war." His father, Alvise, was a farm administrator, a man of some substance, who was able to provide for his family comfortably, until the war took his position and his possessions from him.

First the family moved to Trieste, then Lucca, near Florence, where the elder Andretti found work in a toy factory. These were hard times for everyone in the country. After the war Istria was ceded to Yugoslavia and now no longer is Italian.

Growing up, the Andretti boys were fascinated by cars. Their sister recalls they used to pick up plates off their high-chairs and pretend they were steering wheels. They played with little toy cars on the floor, on table-tops and in bed. Mario remembers gratefully getting a painted box car as a Christmas present. It was flimsy, but the stuff of which dreams are made.

Italy has an unsurpassed auto-racing heritage. More great race drivers came from Italy than from any other European country. They include Tazio Nuvolari, Rudolf Caracciola, and Alberto Ascari, who deserve places on anyone's list of the ten greatest of all time. Another, Ralph De Palma, was born in Italy, but developed in the U. S., blazing a trail for Mario.

In Lucca, there was a garage where local racers prepared their cars. The Andretti twins fastened themselves to this place and were regarded fondly by the proprietors. Men from this garage took the twins to a place near Florence, about seventy miles away, where they could watch a long straightaway and a sweeping turn of the famed Mille Miglia one-thousand-mile road race.

Here they saw the great Ascari duelling the great Juan Manual Fangio of Argentina, as well as Luigi Musso and other outstanding competitors of the time, 1953. "They popped my eyes out," Andretti recalls. "We stood at the end of the straight as it turned into a corner. I've never been able to express it completely, but you can imagine what it meant to me to be that close. Before that time I wanted to be a race driver. After that time, I *had* to be a race driver."

His hero was Ascari. He has never forgotten the way Ascari looked as he sped past in his Lancia. The image of it is fixed in his mind's eye forever. "Take a look at a picture of Ascari," Mario says now. "He's cool. Not leaning forward on the wheel. It's as if he's sitting back and enjoying the ride. I like that. That's the way I like to be."

It might have been foolish for a poor boy to dream of getting a chance to drive an expensive race car, but Mario was blessed by a stroke of unusual good fortune.

In 1954, the Italian government, wishing to develop new racing drivers to replace its aging veterans as its world-wide representatives, adopted a plan conceived by Count Giovanni Lurani, called "Formula Junior Racing," in which teen-agers would be trained and compete in small, less powerful versions of the existing Grand Prix cars.

"It was a sort of Little League of auto-racing, incredibly dangerous, really," Mario recalls with wonder. "Naturally, Aldo and I wanted a part of it. They were accepting drivers of fourteen years of age or older. We were thirteen. We lied to get in. Later, we lied to our parents to stay in. I think we would have done anything to be part of it."

The men at the garage fixed up a simple car for them according to the rules. It was a single-seater powered by a Fiat Topolino engine. They shared it.

They drove on a small track outside of town. They never told their parents they were racing, because their father and mother considered auto-racing a brutal business, did not like it, and never would have permitted their sons to risk themselves in such a dangerous pursuit. When Aldo got injured in a race, the boys said he'd fallen off a truck. When he got burned, they said a box of matches had exploded in his hands. When Mario broke his kneecap, he said he'd fallen on the church steps, of all places.

"All of my relatives over there who say now

they saw me race, they're lying," Mario smiles. "The only one who knew was my old uncle priest. And I told him in confession so he couldn't tell on me." Returning home from races, the twins often paused by the church to get their stories straight. Sometimes their uncle helped them by patching their torn clothes. Then they went home, nursing their secret.

They did well, winning their share. As both recall it, Aldo was a bit better than Mario then, about an inch taller, a little huskier, more aggressive. But, presumably, there was little to choose between them at that point. And that stage of their career did not endure long and ended abruptly. "We ran about twenty-five races, but lots of kids got hurt and some got killed and the people began to kick up a fuss about it and that ended the program," Mario sighs sadly.

They tried motorcycle racing. In one race, a cyclist hit a telephone pole head on. "It split him up," Mario recalls. "I got a good look. I had to wonder if it was what I wanted to do." He thought about it, staying away from races for awhile, but he couldn't stay away long. He was hooked on the narcotic of speed and daring. He watched races and waited until he was old enough to go for a career in Grand Prix racing. Suddenly, then, this was snatched away from him.

In 1959, when Mario and Aldo were nineteen, their parents emigrated to the United States, moving them to Nazareth, Pennsylvania, where they were near relatives who served as their sponsors, and where work had been found for the elder Andretti in a textile factory. At first the twins were crushed, their dreams of gaining racing glory as they knew it smashed. They spoke of returning to Italy when they were able.

Then they found racing in their backyard, a different form of racing than they had ever known, a less glamorous form of racing, but racing—in jalopies and stock cars and midget cars and sprint cars on rutty enclosed oval dirt tracks in front of splintery wooden stands filled with enthusiasts. And not far away, at Langhorne and Trenton, Indianapolis championship cars competed.

As they learned to speak and read English (Mario took a correspondence course to keep up with his classmates), they heard of and read about the Indianapolis 500 and the great drivers of the day, Jimmy Bryan, Tony Bettenhausen, Rodger Ward, Jim Rathmann. Other youngsters were interested in Mickey Mantle, Willie Mays, Johnny Unitas, and Bob Cousy, but the Andretti twins had race drivers as idols and they were old enough now to set out in pursuit of their dreams.

They worked at the garage of their uncle,

Louis, in Nazareth, saved their money, and paid $1,100 for a 1958 Hudson that had been raced by NASCAR star Marshall Teague. He had been killed and his widow sold his car. It was a good car of that racing period. They worked on it, rebuilt it, and went racing in it, learning mechanics and driving skills in the process. Aldo won the first race he entered at the Nazareth Fairgrounds, in 1959, but soon Mario was winning, too. In their first four races, they each won two.

Still, the boys kept their racing secret from their parents, although this time most of their family and friends knew about it. The elder Andretti spoke little English and when his boss at the mill read about the boys and congratulated their father on their success, he was surprised, but supposed he was just being congratulated on having good boys for sons and accepted it.

Mario crashed into a tree once and broke his nose, but made up a story to cover the incident. Then Aldo got hurt, but seriously, and the story they made up did not suffice. In the last race of their first racing season in the U. S., at Hatfield, Pa., Aldo hooked a fence, his car went end over end and he was critically injured. He was taken unconscious from the car and rushed to a hospital, where Mario joined him nervously.

Knowing they were expected home, Mario telephoned his parents that Aldo had fallen from the back of a pickup truck and been injured, but it was nothing serious, nothing to worry about, he would stay by his brother's side, and they did not need to come to the hospital. Then Mario passed a sleepless, lonely, and nervous night in the hospital corridor waiting for word on his brother.

In the morning, hospital authorities demanded to see Aldo's parents. They told Mario if he did not send for them, they would have the police fetch them. Aldo was still unconscious. Reluctantly, Mario called his parents and told them to come to the hospital.

When they arrived, he told them what had happened. The father was furious. The mother wept. It was not just that their sons had been racing for a long time without asking their permission or telling them, but that they had been doing anything in secret, and lying to conceal it. They were an old world family, a close family, with rigid rules about the parents' place as heads of the household. But the racing, itself, was enough.

"Did I raise my sons to have them brought home in a basket?" asked the old man in forlorn anger.

It was thirty days before Aldo revived from his coma. When he came to and was apprised of the situation, his first words to Mario were, "I'm glad, at least, that it was you who had to tell them."

It was forty-five days before Aldo was released to return home. By then the father was secure in the knowledge that his son had survived this close call, but brooded furiously over the risks that had been run, refusing to speak to Mario for awhile.

"It was a bad situation," Mario recalls, "especially in a family such as ours. Soon, I couldn't stand it any longer and moved out." However, his mother, who loved her son and her family more than she hated racing, pleaded with her husband to relent and pleaded with her son to rejoin them. "So I moved back in," Mario recalls.

"I felt bad about what I had done. I still feel bad about that bad time. But I had to have racing. I couldn't lie about that. I couldn't lie any more."

Aldo came home and with Mario began to rebuild their wrecked racer. When the father found out, he was angry again. But now, he saw, there was nothing he could do about it. He could accept the racing, however reluctantly, but he could not surrender his sons. "He could have stopped us," Mario says. "He could have lined us up against a wall and shot us."

Aldo was out for a year, however, and during this time, Mario made enormous progress. When Aldo returned, he was on a lower level than his brother. And he did not do well, crashing repeatedly, struggling, and stalling, while

Mario continued to career upwards in high gear.

In 1961, Mario married Dee Ann, whom he had met when his brother was dating her. In 1962, a son, Michael, was born to them, and in 1963, another son, Jeffrey. Later, in 1969, a daughter was born to them. Meanwhile Aldo had married, too, and begun to raise his own family.

Mario's success and Aldo's failure caused a breach between them. Mario explains sadly, "When he first came back, he pushed too hard, he crashed and crashed and crashed. When I'd tell him I didn't think he should race any more, he'd get very mad and say I was only afraid he'd steal some of my thunder. He couldn't stand it when I was leaving for big races while he stayed home."

After awhile, Aldo moved to Indiana, still chasing his racing dreams. He found work as a mechanic, struggling to support his growing family while going away weekends to race. "I can't tell him not to race any more," Mario said. "I'm afraid to say anything about it to him. He'll do what he wants to do anyway."

As Mario became more and more successful and nationally prominent, Aldo simply could not see why he should not be able to do as well. All his life, he could. And who is to say whether he could or could not? Or should or should not have been able? Who is to specify those fine points of skill and daring and confidence that separate the great ones from the rest? But it is a fact that Mario did well and Aldo did not.

As recently as 1969, Aldo raced and crashed and was seriously hurt. He recovered, his racing future uncertain, but certainly clouded. "I don't know what to say," Mario says. "We no longer are inseparable. I love him. He is a fine person. There are many things he could do and be. Being a racing champion isn't everything. But it is to me, so what can I say?"

As Mario did progress successfully, he could see a softening in his parents' attitude toward racing. Mario points out, "We are a proud people. As I did well, as my picture went up in the barber shops and the saloons in town and began to appear in the newspapers and the national magazines and everyone told my father how proud he should be of me, he began to be proud. It's unbelievable how proud he became.

"At first, he'd never speak to me about racing, but friends and relatives told me he always asked them how I was doing and kept close track of me and spoke with pride of me. Eventually, he agreed to go to a theater in Nazareth to see me race in the Indianapolis 500 on television." Finally, in 1969, they came to see him race in person for the first time in Indy. "Now, I was proud," he says.

Remaining in Nazareth, where he bought land and built a home, Mario became the most prominent figure in his home town.

Even early in his career, Mario was the biggest celebrity in this Pennsylvania Dutch community of some 7,500 residents on the extreme east central New Jersey border, halfway between Philadelphia and Scranton. "I never wanted to leave," Mario shrugs. "You have to have a place that's home, near people you have known for a long time, where it is quiet." His parents still live there. His sister lives with her husband and children in nearby Wayne, New Jersey, where she is a schoolteacher.

In Nazareth, just when he was scaling the heights, a person in a local diner told an interviewer, "Mario Andretti? He's held in pretty high esteem the way I understand it. He's the town hee-row." And the cook said, "All of a sudden everybody's telling me how close they are to him. I've been going to this barber for years and he never mentioned him and now he's his godfather or something, and he's got pictures of him all over."

Mario shrugged when he heard of this and said, "They still aren't beating down the doors."

Soon they would be. Though it didn't come easy. It did come swiftly, but not easily. In 1963 he had been hacking away at the bush leagues of his business, succeeding, but not prospering, getting nowhere, really, and he could see it was time he made a move if he was going to make it as he wanted to make it.

He brooded on it and discussed it with his

wife and finally he asked her permission to quit his job and go to the bigger tracks to seek his fame and fortune. "I didn't have to ask her. It's not that I'm like that," he says. "I wanted to. I thought it only fair. She was young. We had one child and that year we had another. It was my life, but it was hers, too. She was a part of it. If I went hungry, she did. And the kids. If I failed or got hurt, she failed and got hurt. She said to do it. She said to do what I wanted to do."

He sighs, gratefully. "Somewhere along the line almost everyone reaches a point where he has to take a big step, make a big move that will make him or break him. I could have stayed there and lived a normal life, survived, and that would have been it, and not so bad, maybe. But it wasn't what I wanted. I wanted more. My wife had faith in me and was willing to take a chance with me, so I gambled."

were at filling he asked for permission to use. [...]
[...] "The bigger track to [...]
[...] and what "I didn't have to [...]
[...] that. For the [...]" he says. "I [...]

3. The Apprentice

"NO ONE ever taught me anything, not really," Mario Andretti says. "Oh, the odd driver would say the odd thing which might help and a good mechanic like Clint Brawner gave me a few tips which helped, but I used to go to the top men when I first started and I'd ask them questions and they'd look at me like I was crazy and they'd mutter something about doing this or that and they'd walk away and leave me standing there, so I learned not to ask.

"And no one ever gave me anything, either. In the beginning, there were a lot of times that I couldn't get rides and Dee Ann and I would run out of dough. Many times I was refused because I looked like I couldn't get the job done. I'm no Hercules, you know. I'm small and that scared guys off me. There are a lot of guys in this business patting my back now who wouldn't give me a break before.

"I just watched and tried to pick up what I could here and there and took every ride I could get, no matter how poor, and I worked at it. That's the only way to learn this business anyway. It's no good if it's made easy. It's no good if you get a good car right off that makes you think you're better than you are. You just have to drive and learn. It's pretty damn dangerous, but if you survive, you can be a race driver."

After he had gone about as far as he could in jalopies and stock cars on the tracks around Nazareth, winning some twenty feature races in three years, Mario began to move around, shifting into open-cockpit cars—midget cars and sprint cars. A midget car is about half the size of an Indianapolis championship car and a sprint car is about three-fourths the size of an Indy car. They are set up differently, both of them meant to be driven in short races on rough, mostly dirt tracks. Neither of them is enclosed in metal as are stock cars.

"It is a big move from a stock car to an open-cockpit car," Mario smiles. "Maybe it's the biggest move any driver ever makes, and some of them, some good ones, never are willing to make it. In open-cockpit cars, you're out in the open, feeling the wind on your face. You get a far greater sensation of speed than in stock cars. It's easy to run over the exposed wheels and flip. And you know that if you flip, there's nothing over your head. Oh, you got a roll-bar to duck under, but no ton of metal. But if you can drive one car, and if you have the guts, you can drive another."

He drove three-quarter midget cars on indoor board tracks during the winters and summers drove full-sized midget cars and sprint cars on outdoor tracks at Pine Brook, Old Bridge, Olive Bridge, Essex Junction, Rutland, Harrington, Freeport, West Lebanon, Riverhead, Allentown, and Reading throughout New Jersey, New York, Vermont, Delaware, and Pennsylvania, as he beat his way up through the bush leagues of the business. He worked all day at the garage in Nazareth or, later, for a go-kart manufacturer in Easton, then he'd drive to a track at night, getting home around four A.M., then get up around six thirty for another day's work.

"And the safety councils say you're not supposed to drive tired," Mario says.

He did not always win. He did not usually

have a car good enough to win. And the cars he got, he drove hard. "I guess I was a little wild," he admits, laughing. "I've never been afraid, you know, and all I wanted to do was win." But most great drivers were wild at first, cocky and fearless and determined, until this daring enthusiasm is tempered by good judgment. "We all learn," Mario has acknowledged, "that if you can't finish, you can't win." Mario did not have too many wrecks, and car owners and sponsors began to see that if he had a chance to win in a fair car, he would win, so they began to give him better cars. It happened fairly fast, really, faster than it has for most.

In 1963, he won eleven feature races, including a road race on the famed Lime Rock, Connecticut, sports-car course. One day he won several preliminary events and two midget main events at two widely separated tracks. That was Labor Day, 1963. He won at Flemington, New Jersey, in the afternoon, then jumped into the tow-truck and sped over to Hatfield, Pennsylvania, where his brother had been so badly hurt, and won there that night.

He felt he was ready to brave the big-time, so he discussed it with his wife and got her approval and quit his job and hit the road. This was 1964. He got a sprint car ride with Rufus Grey, and he drove some good races, which brought him the offer of a ride in the Trenton 100, the second race of the season on the United States Auto Club championship circuit.

This is the major leagues of American auto racing, one to two dozen races yearly of one hundred miles or more on tracks of a mile or more, including the five hundred on the two-and-one-half-mile Indianapolis Motor Speedway. Points are awarded based on the length of each race and the finish of each driver, and the driver who accumulates the most each season is crowned U. S. king. "I wasn't thinking about any championships that year," Andretti shrugs. "I was just tickled to break into the big time."

However, the Stearly Motor Freight car in which he had to drive his circuit debut at the New Jersey plant was no bargain. On race day it was drizzly and when Andretti first got into the car, he got a shock: He tried the brakes and said, "I can't make these brakes work." A mechanic preparing the old dirt car shrugged and said, "Aw, don't worry, boy, you just have to pump 'em a little." Mario qualified fifteenth fastest, pumping his brakes desperately when he needed them.

It was a wild race, run despite a drizzle because it was being nationally televised. Troy Ruttman, a former Indianapolis champion, skidded upside down and backwards a half-mile in a shower of sparks and flames, but was not seriously hurt. Late in the race, Rodger Ward was leading and closing in on Andretti, ready to lap him, running hard to hold off A. J. Foyt. Ed Kostenuk was ready to pass Andretti first, and as he cut under him sharply, Mario did not give ground. The two cars made contact and were shoved into a spin. Braking to avoid them from behind, Ward stalled. Foyt shot past in the lead and on his way to victory.

As Andretti and Ward climbed from their cars, Rodger offered a few comments to the youngster, suggesting in his own words that if he couldn't keep out of the way perhaps he'd better get the hell off the track. "You drive and you learn," shrugged Mario.

Andretti had more trouble at New Bremen, Ohio, participating in a melee that ironically gave him his greatest break. This was a sprint car race on a savage circuit. Setting the stage, during practice Bobby Black flipped four times and cleared a cement wall, narrowly escaping serious injury. Still, as the race began, Mario was ready to run hard.

On the first lap, in tight traffic, Andretti bumped the rear of Bob Wente's car, blowing out Wente's left rear tire. As Wente fought for control, Andretti went by on the inside. Chuck Hulse tried to follow him through, but ran over Wente's rear wheel and flipped ten times down the track, suffering severe head injuries which would sideline him for the season.

On the restart, Chuck Engel spun, Mickey Rupp slowed to miss him, and Jimmy McGuire, swerving to avoid Rupp, hit Engel's car and flipped, severing his right arm. The race continued, Andretti pressed on and finished third. Leaving the track, he was shaken.

Later, in another sprint car race at Terra Haute, Johnny White vaulted a three-foot retaining wall and was permanently paralyzed. Again, the race went on, Andretti pressed on, and finished high. It was, Mario said, like being at war. You were all in this thing together, taking the same chances. You regretted the serious accidents, but if you wanted to carry on, you endured the thought of them.

Mario carried on, seeking a break that would bring him a ride in which he could be a winner. He was aware that a plush vacancy had been created by the accident of Hulse. Hulse was supposed to drive for sponsor Al Dean and mechanic Clint Brawner in the Dean Van Lines car in the Indy 500, but his mishap left them without a driver as the fraternity convened in Indy in May.

Grey, who had been backing Andretti's sprint car but was not in a position financially to support an Indianapolis project, took Mario to Indy and tried to tout his driver on car owners with vacant cockpits without success. He hardly knew Brawner, but he took Mario into the Dean Van Lines garage and introduced him to Brawner, who, Mario remembers, was still deeply dejected by Hulse's sprint crash. Grey said here's a boy who drives sprints real well, and Brawner said, "Goddamit, sprint's a dirty word in this garage," and turned away from them.

The Dean car went without a driver and Andretti went without a car that month. But he did observe all month, and saw his first 500, which was a frightening one to see.

The European invasion of Indianapolis had begun and many of the veteran drivers were changing over from the front-engine heavyweight roadsters which they had been driving for years to the Grand Prix-styled rear-engine lightweights, which the Europeans drove and which had impressed everyone as the way to go in the future. Still, veterans such as Foyt and Parnelli Jones had not yet given in, and there was considerable indecision.

Scotland's Jim Clark, driving one of Briton Colin Chapman's little Lotus Fords, captured the pole position on the opening day of qualifications with record speeds of 159.377 miles per hour for one lap and an average of 158.828 for four laps. A crowd of nearly 200,000 was on hand, which dazzled Mario. On race day, Memorial Day, more than 300,000 persons streamed into the great arena, which left Andretti hungry for a piece of such spectacular action.

Then, finishing the first lap, a rookie driver, Dave MacDonald, lost control of his new-styled car, scraped an inner wall, splitting his fuel tank, and slid back toward an outer wall as the car exploded into a smoking, flaming inferno.

Several drivers were able to pick their way through the smoke, but veteran Eddie Sachs smashed directly into MacDonald, joining him in a funeral pyre.

The race was halted temporarily, which is done only when it is impossible to continue. Sachs was dead when he was lifted from his car, and MacDonald died in a hospital a little later. By then, the track had been cleared and after one hour and forty-five minutes the tense and dispirited drivers resumed the race. Clark and other leaders broke down. Jones's car exploded in the pits and he narrowly escaped with severe burns. Foyt pressed on to gain his second 500 crown, winning $153,000. Runnerup Rodger Ward collected $56,000. "It was a shaking experience, but if you're a race driver, you're conditioned to it," Andretti sighs.

In Milwaukee, in a one-hundred-miler, Mario was still without a championship ride. He watched as Foyt won again and Jim Hurtubise crashed and suffered nearly crippling burns.

At Terra Haute, in a sprint car race, Andretti lost to Foyt, but hustled him hard, impressing everyone, and after the race, Brawner approached Andretti and asked him if he'd like to come over to his garage and take a better look at his equipment.

Mario says, "I played it cool, saying I might be over the next afternoon. Actually, I was all excited. In major league racing there are only a few outfits worthwhile driving for—the ones that are going to produce a winner. I considered Dean one of these, so I thought maybe I'm finally getting into something good. I was at Brawner's place at five the next morning, waiting for him to open up."

Brawner asked Andretti if he'd like to try the championship car on for size. Mario hopped in. It was big for him, but he said it fit fine. Brawner smiled and said they'd make it fit right. He suggested they skip the next race, a one-hundred-miler on the tough dirt track at Langhorne, and get together for a trial run in the following event, a one-hundred-fifty-miler at Trenton.

Mario agreed to getting together at Trenton but said the heck with skipping Langhorne. He had been talking to the Windmill Truckers crew about driving their car at Langhorne, so he took that ride and finished eighth, as Foyt won again. Then he joined up with Brawner, who was readying a lightweight front-engine car powered by a special Offenhauser engine.

Mario qualified eighth fastest, which was a fine run for a rookie. He recalls, "The last word from Clint was, 'Take it easy and don't worry about a thing; take it easy and learn; we have lots of time.' That's the thing he always said and it played a big part because you knew damn well you're not going to take it easy, you're going to go fast, just as fast as you can go, but boy, it takes an awful lot of the pressure away. Now Clint knows that. He's experienced enough to know that. He figured, 'If this kid is any kind of a driver, he'll still go as fast as he can, but maybe he'll stay out of trouble a little, too.' "

Andretti was running in sixth place until he hit an oil slick and spun, but he maintained control of his car, continued on, and, despite losing a lot of ground, finished tenth. It was not a spectacular showing, but it was a good one. Brawner was satisfied and so was Al Dean, who had observed. Brawner introduced Mario to Dean and recommended Dean take him on permanently. Dean asked Andretti if he wanted to become the team's regular driver and Andretti said he did, so that was that. Later, both Dean and Brawner, who knew the business well and had good eyes for talent, said they were sure they had picked a winner.

At Springfield, in a one-hundred-miler on the dirt, Mario qualified ninth and finished sixth, as Foyt won his seventh straight championship race. Bill Horstmeyer, making his first championship circuit start, hit a rail, flipped end over end, landed upside down in flames, and was killed. At Milwaukee, in a two-hundred-miler on the paved oval before more than 30,000 fans, Parnelli Jones outran Rodger Ward for the victory as Foyt broke down. Here, Mario made his greatest impression, finishing a fine third. He won $4,100. But the big money was beckoning now.

Andretti's engine stalled in a one-hundred-miler on the dirt at DuQuoin, Illinois, his face was bloodied by a rock sucked up in the Hoosier Hundred on the dirt at the Indiana State Fairgrounds, and his engine blew up in the Trenton 200. He had run out of the top ten through three straight frustrating events. At Sacramento, everything stayed in one piece and Mario finished eighth. And in the season finale at Phoenix, Mario finished eighth again. Later, Bobby Marshman crashed and was fatally burned while testing tires at Phoenix.

It had been a promising, but unspectacular first year on the championship trail for Andretti, but this is a tough tour, which has smashed the hopes of many fine hopefuls and broken or destroyed countless competitors. Along the way, he drove successfully in enough sprint car races to finish in third place in points among USAC sprint drivers. He won one major sprint test, the longer than usual one-hundred-lap, fifty-mile Pat O'Connor–Joe James Memorial Race on the half-mile paved track at Salem, Indiana, where the course is so steeply banked, "it like to scare me out of my wits," says Mario.

In all, he earned for his teams $18,466. When the season was over, almost everyone could see

Andretti was on the brink of big things. You just don't get there in auto-racing all at once, but Andretti was arriving fast. Dean figured he was due for a break and maybe Mario was it. "He might be the one to win Indy for me," the neat, fiftyish little moving man said. Dean had been running race cars at Indianapolis and on the championship circuit since 1954, investing the money he made from his successful San Diego–based business in pursuit of his business. "I make money moving furniture and lose money moving race cars," he says. "I cheat on my wife and family, not with fast women, but with fast cars. I got hooked on racing as a young man, and as soon as I could afford it, I got into it. It is not a good business, but it is an exciting one. And it won't let me go."

All along Brawner had been his mechanic and the chief of his team, assisted since 1954 by the brilliant young Jim McGee. Together they had given opportunity to some of the best young drivers—A. J. Foyt, Bob Sweikert, Jimmy Bryan, and Eddie Sachs among them. Bryan won three national titles for Dean and Brawner in their cars and finished second in the 500 for them, but he won the 500 for another sponsor and mechanic after he left them. Foyt won national titles and the 500 for others after he left them. Sweikert won both after leaving Dean. Sachs had come closest to winning the 500 for them, leading with three laps to go in 1961 when he pitted to replace a worn tire and finished second behind Foyt. Now, Sachs had been killed at Indy after leaving them.

"I am proud that no driver has ever been killed in one of my cars, thanks, of course, to Clint Brawner," Dean sighed. "I am not a bloodthirsty boxing manager sending my tigers out to get hurt. I have never talked anyone into driving a race car. I pick the best drivers I can find, and send them out in the best equipment I can get, prepared by the best mechanic I know. For a fellow who has been in this business as long as I have been, this is a remarkable record of safety. We go to win, but never at the expense of safety. It is not a safe business and we have been lucky, but we have also been careful.

"I don't know why good drivers leave us after we give them a break. I think they think we're too cautious. Or jinxed. We win more than our share of races and titles, but we've never won the big one, Indy. We almost did with Sachs. I still run that race over and over in my mind and I still can't believe we lost it. I don't blame Eddie for coming in, but it hurts to think about it. Maybe Andretti will win it for us. He seems like a little tiger."

In Phoenix, Brawner said, "I was a race-driver myself until I went diving into an old pond that was too shallow and broke my fool neck. So I became a mechanic. And I'm a good one. Like Dean says, our record of safety is outstanding. I've never had a driver killed or even seriously hurt in one of my cars. Guys who drove for me have been killed in other guys' cars but not mine. Eddie Sachs was killed in someone else's car this year. You better believe it broke me up, but at least my conscience was clear."

The tall, gaunt, weatherbeaten Arizonan sighed and said, "It's debatable whether Eddie should have come into the pits at Indy in 1961 or taken a chance and kept going. Maybe the tire would have held up three more laps and maybe it wouldn't have. You don't get that close to the big one very often and maybe you should take a chance to win it, and maybe you shouldn't. But it was his decision to make and he made it. I guarantee you if he'd not come in and that tire had gone and he had been killed, I'd have felt a lot worse about it than I do now about losing.

"Our cars finish and they win more than their share. These cars don't finish by accident, you know. A lot of know-how and sweat goes into them. But you don't win without a good driver. We've had good drivers. Some of 'em didn't want to play it safe, but that's the way we operate. They won plenty our way, but they didn't win Indy, so I guess they figured they'd shop around for something a little better.

Maybe someone offers 'em a little more money than Dean does, so they go to someone else. It's all right. It's a business, a dangerous business. A guy's got a right to do the best he can for himself. It's just that his judgment may not always be right."

He shook his head, looking down at his calloused, but sensitive hands. He said, "I think Mario has a good chance with us. And we've got a good chance with him. He's young, but I'd rather have a young guy with promise who's willing to learn than an old guy who has had his best days and thinks he knows it all. Mario's got a lot to learn, of course, but he's learning fast. He's small, but that doesn't matter. It's how you handle a car that matters, and his size doesn't seem to bother him. The lighter the car, the faster it goes. Mario saves me fifty to seventy-five pounds over some drivers.

"There's a lot of things you can do to a race car to set it up for different drivers and different tracks and different races. When you practice, you sort it all out so the car is set up best for that driver on that track that day. Mario knows cars and he helps us sort ours out. Eddie Sachs could drive, but he didn't know beans about cars. A. J. Foyt can drive and he knows as much as any mechanic, but he can't work with a mechanic, he wants to do it all himself. Mario helps you, but he lets you do your job."

"You learn," Mario said. "My first car, that

old Hudson, was no junker. A lot of thought and work went into it. We learned about springs and shock absorbers. After running a while, you get to know what you want and you set up the equipment where it feels best. A lot of drivers go like hell when the car's right, but when it isn't right, they can't help themselves. Some of us can help the mechanic find out what's wrong. This is not something you are born with, it's a talent you acquire.

"I like to be around when my car is being set up, especially if we're running on a new track. Then the crew and I put our heads together and try new things, as I want to know what's being tried. That way, you know what to change when it's needed. You know, there are some big-time drivers with whom I race who simply pull in after a few laps and say, 'This thing runs like a pig.' Well, the poor mechanic has to guess what the trouble is. You've got to know what's happening with a racing car—it's doing this or that. Then your crew can get things working properly. It's like telling a doctor where the pain is before he examines you."

Some cars simply would not be good enough no matter what was done to them. Such as Mario's first sprinter. "It was a real box," he recalls. "Man, I had trouble sorting it out. I just didn't know which way it was going to go. One of the negative factors in my early sprint career was that I couldn't get a really good ride.

Later, I got into a really good midget. Before getting into this machine, I had just been running around the track, not really getting any place. Now, I started winning. It was a whole new picture. It gave me a lot of confidence.

"Before, when I was driving a 'box,' I wondered whether it was me or the car that was bad. When I started in those early sprints, to me anything that had four wheels, a racing-car look, and a steering wheel was a real race car. I was just glad to sit in it. I never really worried about how the thing actually worked. Finally, when I sat in something really good, the guys that used to whoosh by me, those you wouldn't see until after the race—now these were the same guys I was now running in contention with. It was a whole new bag. Things really started working."

It was a rough school, one in which the hard knocks may prove fatal. What the other drivers would not teach Mario off the track, they tried to teach him on it. "Some guys want to stick you in the wall to teach you," Mario says. They tested him, seeing if he'd give ground when they pressed him while passing him, or dropped in front of him, cutting him off. "They find out quickly if you have the guts to win," Mario says. "Anyone can learn to race. Or almost anyone. But not many can win. They find out fast whether you have the guts to win. You got to have the skill. And you have to have the guts."

He was sitting in the pits in the sunshine. He said, "I'm not afraid on a race track in a race car. I'm comfortable there. The thing is, there's nothing in the world I'd rather be doing than what I'm doing. I'm doing what I love best. I'm good at it and I'm going to be better. I know I have a lot to learn. I will learn. I'll be the best before I'm done," he said very seriously, his eyes hidden behind those sunglasses.

4. The Champion

AFTER Mario Andretti hit the top, a representative of an outboard motor company approached him and asked him if he'd like to try his hand at the throttle of a high-powered hydroplane? Mario said he would like the challenge. Fine, the man said. And, by the way, Mario did know how to swim, didn't he? Yes, Mario said, he knew how to swim. Fine, the man said,

and how long could he hold his breath
under water? Mario paused. "How long
does it take to fish me out of the water?"
he asked.

By then, Andretti had decided to pass up the
boat racing for awhile. But he did drive everything else he could find to race. Once, his manager, Chuck Barnes, suggested that Mario
would be unwise to risk running a minor sprint
car race at Eldora just before the Indianapolis
500. Mario was determined to run, anyway. "It
doesn't make any sense," he admitted, "but
that's the way I feel about it, and that make's
sense. I can't make them understand, so I just
don't talk about it. But if you start thinking
you may get hurt, you may as well get out of
racing."

Mario has said, "Racing wouldn't be racing
without the thrills. I don't want to do something with no risk in it. I think the risk thrills
the crowd. But I don't think any fans really
want any driver to get hurt. In 1964 when that
terrible fire happened at Indianapolis, I was in
the stands and I don't think there was a single
person who enjoyed the race after that."

He was shaken when his best friend, Billy
Foster, was killed in a race. He says, "He was
my best friend and toughest competitor. I could
see so much ability in that man. We used to

41

enjoy a lot of things. His wife and mine were great friends, too. It's a hell of a problem." Yet he went on driving.

"You have to be a dedicated person," he said. "You have to want it in a bad way. Then you have to have ability. You have to be brave, but you have to have sense. When you're a driver, you're playing with your life. You have to drive not only with your foot, but with your brain. A lot of drivers are smart enough to know how to go the quickest with the least amount of danger.

"I'm no fool. When we talk about this, we're not only talking about driving, we're talking about equipment failure. Things can happen that can't be helped. And to be good, a race driver has to take chances. I know that I've taken chances. But I know what I'm doing when I take a chance. The guy who has confidence in his car and pushes it to the limits, that's a real race driver. The foolish ones who don't know what they're doing you can put a number on."

Prior to the 1965 season, USAC made it mandatory to carry rubber-bladder fuel-cells inside the fuel tanks, which reduced the possibility of explosive fires, even when the tanks were split, thus encouraging the rush to the rear-engine lightweight cars. Clint Brawner and Jim McGee rebuilt the old roadster, lightening it greatly. They then took the pattern of

Grand Prix champion Jack Brabham's rear-engine car and fashioned their own rear lightweight from it, which Brawner called "The Hawk." This was the first car that had been built especially for Andretti, with a cockpit designed from his small frame.

However, it was not ready for the opening of the season and Andretti went racing in the Phoenix 100 in the rebuilt roadster. "It may be outdated, but it still works awfully good," he said. "This car is so sensitive that if a pickup truck drives across the track, I can feel where it crossed." Facing the fanciest in new equipment, he took his antique out and outran everyone for sixty-five lamps until Johnny Rutherford spun around him and smacked him into the infield. By the time Andretti resumed, he had to hustle to gain sixth place. Don Branson won. Foyt was just recovering from a serious crackup at Riverside, California, three months earlier and was out of it.

Going into Trenton for another one-hundred-miler, Andretti was discussed as a new sensation who might be a threat at Indianapolis, although this would be his first race in the 500, where rookies never win, and where Andretti was considered a rookie. In the last tuneup, Andretti ran second to Jim McElreath. Rain fell from the fifteenth lap on until the race was called after eighty-seven miles, and Andretti's old roadster was not as well suited to a slick track as the nimble lightweights, so his showing was impressive.

Then, Indianapolis. Mario got there before his new car did. A week before, in fact. While others were practicing to points of perfection, he sat idle. As a rookie he had to take a difficult test in which he had to run forty laps at specific speeds without a speedometer while negotiating the course under the stern observation of veteran drivers and officials. Many fine drivers have flunked this test and been sent back for more experience. Eddie Sachs flunked it. And Mario had to pass it before he could even practice at high speed. And he never had driven a rear-engine car before.

Nervously, he paced through the pits. "I'm going to get out there as soon as the car arrives. I want to get that rookie test over with— boom!" Publicly, he expressed confidence. Privately, he admitted, "I'm going out of my mind waiting." He had never even driven the car he would have to test in and then drive the toughest of races in. Most observers assumed his chances for a good showing had been destroyed by the delay.

The car came and Mario vaulted into it. He took it right out on the track. "I felt so secure in it, it worried me," he said. Swiftly, he asked for his test. Boom, he passed it. Officials said they had never seen a more perfect test, or a rookie who adapted to this tricky track so swiftly. Soon, Mario was hurtling around the track at 160 miles per hour, almost as fast as the fastest.

A. J. Foyt, Parnelli Jones, and Rodger Ward nervously tried out new lightweights. The cars of Foyt and Jones came apart and crashed, but the drivers survived. Their cars were repaired. Ward's car seemed to baffle him and he couldn't get it up to speed as the first of the four qualifying days approached. The pole position is won on opening day. The fastest secure the top starting positions, while the rest struggle to make the field of thirty-three starters. Without a good starting position, it is difficult to win this race. Usually, the front-runners are too swift to be caught. Andretti eyed a top position.

On the first Saturday of time trials, a crowd of more than 200,000 persons poured onto the grounds. Andretti had drawn an early run and he seemed calm as the time drew near. It is his way. Inside, he admitted, he was nervous. "Here I was ready to go against the greatest drivers in the fastest cars. No traffic. Just solo runs. One by one. But I'd be compared to them. Everyone expected a lot of me. I didn't like it, but I felt the pressure. I'd been doing fine. The track didn't seem tough. But now the money was on the line."

He strapped himself into his new car and sped away. His first lap was the fastest ever run at Indianapolis, 159.179 miles per hour. The crowd came to its feet, cheering him on. The second lap was a tick slower, 158.618. The third lap, a tick slower yet, 158.200. His pit crew waved him on. The record remained within reach. Mario kept his foot to the floorboard and steered with determination. On his last lap, he set a new record for one lap, 159.405, and completed a new record average of 158.849 for four.

He coasted into the pits, hearing the cheers, and waving and grinning to the crowd and his crew, led by Brawner, who came running to him on wings of wonder. "Hey, hey, hey," Brawner shouted, embracing him. "It was some kind of thrill," Mario recalls.

Even as Mario was being congratulated, Jimmy Clark sped his Lotus Ford out and around at 160.973 for one lap and 160.729 for four, smashing through the 160-mile-per-hour barrier at the Speedway and surpassing Andretti's short-lived standard. Then tough Foyt slammed out and hurried a fast lap of 161.985 and an average for four of 161.233, raising the records higher yet.

No one remaining could top this, though Dan Gurney averaged 158.898 to squeeze Mario out of the front row and into the inside slot on the second row of three cars. Parnelli Jones was fifth fastest at 158.2625 to fill the slot alongside Andretti. Mario's ill-fated pal, Billy Foster, completed the row at 158.416.

Qualifying continued on Sunday. Then, practice resumed. Jones's car came apart again, and he crashed. Again, he escaped serious injury. Again, his car had to be rebuilt. On the second Saturday of qualifying, Ward crashed. Overnight, his car had to be rebuilt. On the second Sunday, the last day of qualifying, Ward failed to make it.

Only fine differences separate the cars that contest for honors at Indianapolis. Ward's full ten-mile trial consumed only two seconds more than that of the thirty-third fastest qualifier, but that was two seconds too many to make the race. He averaged only two seconds per two-and-one-half-mile lap slower than Foyt, who sat on the pole in glory. But after fourteen consecutive years in the race and two victories, Ward was out of it.

He sat in his car with his head hung in disappointment as the photographers and writers moved around him to prepare his obituary as a champion. His failure, along with the crashes of Foyt and Jones, seemed to symbolize the ending of the reigns of the old guard who had dominated Indy with their old ways. Foyt was on the pole, but few felt he could contain Clark over the full race.

Andretti symbolized the new era, an Italian-born racer in a race that seemed destined to be dominated by Europeans, or at least European-style drivers. His idols had been road racers. He had learned to race on road courses in

Grand Prix-styled cars. But this was deceptive. Mario had matured as a racer in American-styled midget cars and sprint cars and stock cars on oval tracks, many of them dirt tracks. It was true that in the immediate future most of Indy's hottest newcomers would be road racers from sports-car circuits, but Mario really had been cut from the old cloth—a sprinter from dirt ovals, a link between past and future.

On race day the 300,000 cram the grounds. Bands march. The cars are pushed to the track, the drivers and their crews stand by them, and a thousand persons with official badges swarm around them. The national anthem is sung. And "Back Home Again In Indiana." And "Taps" is played. Bombs go off. Balloons are released. The drivers climb into their cars and strap themselves in. For a rookie like Andretti, it is a tremendous moment, full of fears and uncertainties and ambitions. The fans look at the cars and wonder which will win and which may not return.

Tony Hulman, the president of the Speedway, takes a microphone and says, "Gentlemen . . . start your engines!" And the electric starters are thrust into the cars and they rev up in a sudden roar of sound and begin to drift away, circling the track, settling into their places behind the pace car. Andretti leans back, trying to relax, guiding his car carefully. The pace car thunders into the mainstretch and swings off into the pits as the eleven rows of racers pick up the pace. The green flag is unfurled and the powerful cars accelerate into the first turn in a roaring, smoking, stinking tangle of traffic, and through it safely, somehow, and on into the race.

It is a long, hard race, equal to 50,000 miles of highway wear and tear on the average car. These precisely built and tuned creations are pushed to their limits. The crews have made experienced guesses on how best to balance them and the amounts of fuel to give them and the number of pit stops to be made. Every second spent in the pits is precious. Many races are lost in the pits. Many races are lost through mechanical breakdowns. Others are lost through driver error.

Andretti, counseled by Brawner, sought to restrain himself, driving carefully while he mastered the event. Conservatively, he settled into a spot in the front third of the pack for the first third of the race, then began to move up. Meanwhile, Clark, as good as the best driver, and with the best car, was pulling away from Foyt, Jones, and Gurney. Gurney's car broke down at 150 miles and Foyt's at 300 miles. Bud Tingelstad crashed the wall in the only accident of an unusually safe 500, but was not hurt.

Jones and Andretti both began to experience problems with their cars. Jones's fuel lines were faulty and his car kept drying out and he had to keep ducking into the pits to feed it. Andretti's car had been set up straight up and down, in contrast to most Indy cars which are weighted to the left to compensate for the 800 left turns. Centrifugal force on the turns kept driving the fuel from the tanks on the left side of Andretti's car to the right side, throwing it out of balance and several times nearly pitching it up into an outside wall. "It became a struggle just to keep it going straight," he commented.

Soon, there was no question of catching Clark, but only hope of catching Jones in second place. Despite their problems, Jones, the old master, and Andretti, the new genius, were out-driving the survivors, providing the huge throng with its only excitement.

After three hours and nineteen minutes, having averaged 150 miles per hour and having led for 190 of the 200 laps, Clark took the checkered flag two full laps in front of his troubled pursuers. Two minutes later, Jones, almost out of fuel, came wildly down the stretch, swerving from side to side in an effort to toss the last drops of fuel into his engine. One hundred yards behind him, Andretti, arm-sore from wrestling his mishandling monster, came on.

Jones made it, running dry as he coasted past the finish line. Then came Andretti, accepting congratulations with a wistful, but disappointed, smile.

At the victory dinner, Clark picked up a check for $166,621 for his team, Jones one for $64,661, and Andretti one for $42,551. Andretti also was voted "rookie of the year," entitling him to a $500 check, and an assortment of prizes including a year's supply of meat. "Now, Dee Ann and I will not go hungry," he said, grinning.

He was disappointed that he had not won, yet in this case he was thrilled by the laurels heaped on him and satisfied by his performance under the circumstances. "I felt good about it. It's rare that a rookie does as well," he said.

Brawner was less pleased. On behalf of the Dean team he claimed second place, filing a protest that Jones had been illegally restarted with a push in the pits during one of his stops. There seemed some merit to his claim, but it was disallowed. Brawner expected it and accepted it, shrugging something about the power of Jones's powerful boss, J. C. Agajanian, a respected veteran in USAC circles. "One thing," Brawner said, "Andretti showed me he can beat this place."

It is a hard place to survive, much less conquer. The track is a difficult one, composed of two long straightaways of five-eights of a mile each, two short straightaways of one-eighth of a mile each, and four corners of a quarter-mile each. It is barely banked, so the cars get little help negotiating the turns. It is paved and soon gets slick with oil thrown off by the cars. It must be driven smoothly. Every mistake is costly. The differences between cars are measured in split seconds and the stakes are so high the pressure on the competitors is enormous.

"There are harder tracks, I think, really," Andretti says. "There are shorter tracks with tighter turns, for example. But we don't have to drive them as long or at such speed. One of the things that makes this track tough is it is very difficult to find where you can pick up fractions of seconds on your rivals. The top cars are usually fairly equal. You have to find some edge out on the track and those seconds you want hide from you out there.

"I learned a lot in my first experience there and I immediately took tire-testing jobs for Firestone to learn more. It is not the money, but the experience you gain on the track that makes these testing jobs so precious. It is a dangerous place, of course, because of the speed and the intensity of the competition, but these are the best cars and the best drivers, so it is no more dangerous than shorter, slower races with inferior equipment on inferior tracks against many mediocre drivers. People build up all sorts of mental blocks about this place, but it's just a place and it can be beaten."

Faith in his future here strong, Mario moved on his way along the championship trail. At Milwaukee, Jones won with Andretti fourth. At Langhorne, Andretti appeared on his way to his first title triumph as he led Jim McElreath after seventy-five miles of bitter battling. A multi-car crackup and fiery aftermath, which cost Mel Kenyon some fingers, put the field into a slow procession under the yellow caution flag for awhile. McElreath caught Andretti napping on the restart, surging past him, and Mario was unable to recapture the lead by the one-hundred-mile finish. Live and learn.

At Trenton, the rear end of Mario's car came apart in practice and he was sidelined as Foyt won. Finally, in the Hoosier Grand Prix on the road course at Indianapolis Raceway Park, Andretti broke through for his first victory on the circuit. He qualified fastest at 111.6 miles per hour, then swapped the lead back and forth with Foyt in a furious run that had the crowd standing and screaming. Foyt took the lead at one point as Mario ran off the course briefly. But unable to make a pit stop because of the pressure being applied by Andretti, Foyt ran out of fuel on the final lap, Mario sped past him to win.

It had been a brutal race in which Norman Hall flipped through five steel posts and levelled more than twenty-five feet of guard rail in an accident which cost him a foot. It had been the first road race on the championship trail since the Vanderbilt Cup Races of more than a quarter-century earlier, though only the first of many that would begin with the arrival of the

Grand Prix-styled cars, and many deemed it appropriate that Italian-born, Grand Prix-inspired Andretti should win it. He averaged 101 miles per hour for the winding struggle and picked up $4,350 for his team.

At Atlanta, on the one- and one-half-mile, steeply-banked southern stock-car course, Johnny Rutherford outran Andretti by a lap as Foyt's car broke down. At Langhorne, McElreath won as Andretti's seat bracket snapped and he was tossed around in his cockpit as he sped to a difficult fourth-place finish.

At Milwaukee, Andretti and Dan Gurney ran side by side, wheel by wheel for 125 miles in one of the most exciting and entertaining duels of the season. Eventually, both dropped out with mechanical troubles, and Joe Leonard won, but Mario remembers the race with pleasure.

"I'll bet he was alongside of me a dozen times," he says. "I mean clean alongside of me. Usually, if a guy plays me short, I'll play him short right back. It's a natural thing. But when Gurney and I went into the turns, I went on the outside and he had all the racing room possible to give a man. We talked about it later. We both really enjoyed it."

This was pure racing, two intense competitors, one experienced, the other one comparatively inexperienced, but both with respect for each other's skill and judgment, feeling safe and comfortable competing side by side at great speed.

Despite only one victory, Mario had been placing consistently high, piling up points and pulling further and further ahead in the championship standings. Another steady finisher, Jim McElreath, ranked second. Four-time champion Foyt had broken down repeatedly and needed a number of victories to vault into the lead unless Andretti began to run out of the money. Usually, the Indianapolis 500 victory, worth 1,000 points to the winner, twice as many as a 250-mile victory and five times as many as a one-hundred-mile victory, gives the winner a big head start on the title run, but this year's 500 champion, Clark, was back in Europe, and Andretti was rolling towards glory.

Foyt did win the Springfield 100, with Andretti third. Andretti was well on his way to winning the Milwaukee 200 when his engine blew, but Gordon Johncock snatched the victory from Foyt. At DuQuoin, Mario's car threw oil all over the place and he had to give up, but Foyt finished only third to Don Branson and was eliminated from title contention. Still, Foyt bounced back to win his thirtieth championship race in the Hoosier Hundred at Indianapolis as Andretti, placing second, came within a few points of clinching the crown.

At Trenton, as Foyt won easily, Mario, struggling far back, spun a contender, Bobby

Unser, out of contention and finished thirteenth, but backed into the title. Jim McElreath settled for a third-place spot without enough points at stake in the remaining races to overhaul Andretti. "I'm sorry I had to spoil the race for Unser, but I'm glad I won the championship," said a weary Andretti later, as others griped at the way he had won the crown.

In Sacramento for the Golden State 100, veteran drivers speculated about Andretti's tactics which had netted him only one victory, and frowned about the fortunes which had permitted the novice to win the driving title with just that one victory. Jones, who never had won the title, said, "There is no questioning his ability, but he may be overextending himself. The longer you run, the more natural this thing is for you. I don't think it's natural for him yet. I just hope he realizes how dangerous this business is."

Two-time champion Ward said, "He should become one of the great ones, but frankly I think he drives a little harder than he should with his lack of experience. He's gotten into a little trouble here and there. Fortunately, it hasn't been serious, but he's been a little lucky." Four-time king Foyt said, "He's good. We'll have to wait and see just how good he really is."

It is a fact that Andretti had been lucky to win the one race he won, when Foyt ran out of fuel near the finish. However, it is also a fact that in races in Phoenix, Trenton, Milwaukee, and Langhorne, Mario was unlucky in losing as he suffered car failures in contests he seemed likely to win. "Sure I'd have liked to have won more races, but I won the title so that wasn't bad for beginners," Mario said.

He sat in his motel room, relaxing in sports clothes. His wife had taken their sons for a walk. He had won $70,000 in purses for his team during the season. He had the average contract which called for him to receive fifty per cent of all winning prizes and forty per cent of all other monies won, but he was now in a position to demand a guaranteed salary of $100,000 or more and to command lucrative endorsement money from automotive firms and fat fees for public appearances. He had taken on a business manager, Chuck Barnes of Sports Headliners, who also managed Foyt and Jones and later would manage football star O. J. Simpson. Mario's fame was growing and his fortunes were spiraling upwards.

He had bought land to build a home for himself and his family in Nazareth, a new Mustang and a station wagon, and a trailer so his family could accompany him on tour. Dee Ann came in and said, "I like the travelling and I like the racing. At first it was more than a little hectic. We didn't have much money and we did have babies. Now it's not so bad. We have money and the kids are older. I worry about Mario, of course. I've been badly scared a couple of times. But I'd rather be at races watching him than off somewhere wondering about him. And I do have confidence in him and I am proud of him. Eventually, when the boys are in school, I may have to stay home with them. Now, as long as he wants us, I want to be with him."

"Sure I want them with me," Mario said. "She's had to cope with terrible problems while I was on the way up and yet she encouraged me to go on and she comforted me when I was depressed and she held things together, and now that I seem to be reaching the top, I want her alongside me. It's easy when you can afford to go first class, and I can. I want her to share in everything good that comes to me. It takes a special kind of woman to be a race-driver's wife, and she's a champ."

He is a handsome little fellow, with a full head of dark, wavy hair, saucer-sized, brooding eyes and fine features. He is pursued by the girls who chase the hero drivers. Chuck Barnes said, "The ladies think he's the greatest thing since sliced bread. This could lead to trouble, but Mario won't let it. I don't think anything could spoil him." Al Dean said, "He loves it— the attention—but he's a clean kid, as straight as a string, with a lovely wife and fine boys, and despite the incredible temptations to dissipate, I think he'll maintain his balance."

Andretti, who smokes only occasionally and sips little more than a glass of wine now and then, simply is not the hell-raiser some of the brawny, brawling drivers are. "I'm human," he said, smiling, "but you can either be a playboy or a winner, and I'd rather win than have fun. Let's say my idea of having fun is to win a race. I only won one big one this year, but I led a lot. You can win anything you can lead, and I'm gonna' start winning."

He seemed sensitive to criticism. "For six straight years, Foyt or Ward had won every championship. Jones never won one. They're good, but possibly they're a little jealous of me right now." He shrugged. "I drive hard, sure. But you have to drive hard to win. And it's my style. I drive into the corners deeper than most guys. I hit the brake hard, but I get off it fast and hit the accelerator hard. Sometimes I've still got my foot on the brake when I begin to accelerate. I try to make my passes on the straights. I just try to get around a little quicker than the next guy.

"Anyone who says I got into a lot of trouble on the track this year is wrong. I was in hardly any trouble. I was in some. You can't run fast in traffic a whole season without getting into some trouble. In Terra Haute, I was crowded into a wall and my car began to climb it. That baby really took off and I thought it was the end for awhile, but I slid back down and stopped on all fours. If you walk away from it, you laugh about it, you push it away and forget it.

"At Trenton, I was out of it, but still charging. Maybe I shouldn't have been, but that's my way. I tried to get underneath Bobby Unser to pass him and clipped him and knocked him out of the race. I felt like crawling in a hole. It shouldn't have happened. He didn't say anything to me, but I know how he felt. It happened to me, too. I had Phoenix won when Johnny Rutherford spun me out. And I felt angry about it, but I didn't say anything to him. They talk big about sportsmanship, but no one gives anyone anything.

"A couple of times the cars betrayed me. At Indy, I had all I could do to hold her on the track. At Trenton, the rear end of the car gave way and I found myself without any control of her. I ripped out a piece of fence before I slid sideways to a stop in the infield. This wasn't much for a whole season's racing. Maybe I've been a little lucky. But I think I've been a little good, too. They say I may scare myself out of it when I have my first bad accident, but I haven't been scared by the accidents I have had, and if I have my way I'll never have a really bad one."

He lay back on the bed and cupped his hands behind his head and stared at the ceiling. He said, "They worry about my inexperience, but I've been driving since I was thirteen and I came up the hard way. I may be new to the big time, but not to racing. Miracles don't happen. I finished most of my races. If a newcomer out-performs veterans it can only be because he has the ability to do it. If I overdrive, it's dangerous not only to myself, but to others; I know that. But if I had overdriven, I would not have done what I have done. In fact, I would probably not be here at all.

"I did what I did with a lot of help. I had good cars and a good crew. Except at Indy and one or two places, the cars were real good. They can be better and will be. The crew will see to that. Or else I'll go someplace else. I'd do this thing if there wasn't a dime in it, but there's a lot of dollars in it and so I want my share. Anyone who does this thing and doesn't get rich at it is a fool. As long as Dean gives me good cars and good help and the best deal I can make, I'll stay with him. He's been a good boss, but I'm not married to him. If I can do better some-where else, I'll go. This isn't a game I'm play-ing. I put my life on the line and I want it to be worthwhile."

In the lobby, Dean said, "I have had the greatest of 'em driving for me and Mario rates with any of them. It broke my heart when the others saw fit to leave me. I don't think Mario will leave me. We have a contract that says he won't. I don't rely on promises any more. Mario is hungry. I nicknamed him 'Tiger.' He's after something and he won't let go until he gets it. He won the national title and he'll win others. He wants Indianapolis and he'll win it. It's my dream to win there. I have tried so long and suffered so many near misses. Maybe Mario will win it for me."

In the coffee shop, Brawner wrapped his hands around a steaming mug of coffee and said, "Mario is something else. He has the big boys nervous. He goes into the turns so far, he almost gets lost. He really lets it all hang out. But he rarely seems to lose control for even a second. He's getting very good very fast. As we tailor-make some cars just right for him, he'll be very hard to beat before long."

He sighed. "I feel very close to him," he said. "I count on him. He counts on me. Drivers and mechanics have to be able to count on each other. We depend on each other. So I take care of him. Mario's wife's a good girl. She doesn't butt in. This is important. Drivers' wives can get in the way. She's all right. She worries, sure, but she doesn't worry us about it. She lets us do our jobs without getting in the way. Travelling together, we're a family. We feel for each other. We share victory and we share defeat. It's a very delicate arrangement.

"I wouldn't be surprised if Andretti leaves us sooner or later, however. Others have, why shouldn't he? I may leave Dean myself one of these days. I've thought about it every year.

Why? Money. If you get a better deal, you go."

In the bar, the music was banging away and the cocktail glasses were clattering and the dolls were giggling and the drivers were bragging. In their room, Mario and Dee Ann Andretti had dressed and welcomed the baby-sitter and were on their way out to eat with friends.

They passed a quiet evening and returned early. Mario slept soundly and got up early. He ate a breakfast of ham and eggs and toast and got to the track early. He sat in the morning sunshine and waited while his men worked on his car. The crowd filled up the stands and Mario went out and raced. He duelled Don Branson for the lead up to the halfway point, but Branson had more this day and pulled away. Foyt had started far back and gradually worked his way up until he caught and passed Andretti with eighteen miles to go. Mario finished third.

He packed his gear and loaded the trailer and started out with his wife and sons for Phoenix. Here, he set a record for a mile track in qualifying with a trial run of 121.4 miles per hour. He led the two-hundred-miler for 185 miles, pressed fiercely by Foyt all the way. Then, trying to lap an also-ran, Dempsey Wilson, he tangled with Wilson's car, knocking part of his car's tail section loose, and slowed down as Foyt sped past to win. Afterwards, he griped, "Wilson didn't give me room. He chopped down on me in the turn as if he was racing me, although he was out of it." Then he shrugged and went to sit on the pit wall.

His season had ended and he had won $96,407 and the national title by winning one race, placing second five times, third three times, and fourth twice in sixteen events. Foyt won five races, but had not done well in most of the others. Mario was the fourth national champion sponsored by Al Dean and guided by Clint Brawner on the Dean Van Lines team. He was the first foreign-born champion since English-born Henry Banks won the honors in 1950 and the first Italian-born driver to dominate American racing since Ralph DePalma fifty years earlier. And Andretti was, at twenty-five, the youngest driver ever to win the U. S. crown.

Andretti was the fourth driver to win "Rookie of the Year" honors at Indianapolis and the national title in the same season. Johnny Parsons, who was the last to do it before Andretti, said, "It's a tremendous thing for anyone to do. You just can't believe how tough it is. No one gives you a thing. Andretti did it and I'm sure he had to earn it." Henry Banks, now a USAC official, said, "He is an exceptionally impressive champion." Sam Hanks, a former Indianapolis and national champion and a USAC official, said, "He is the best newcomer in years. I imagine he can see his limits better than anyone else. His success proves he hasn't overextended himself. He has drive. He also has an exceptional personality. He's very clean-cut and reliable. He could be quite a credit to racing."

Rival car owners lauded him. Andy Granatelli said, "He's some *paisan*. I'm proud of him. I'd sign him in a second." J. C. Agajanian said, "Notice how he walks. He's short and has short legs, but he always strides out ahead of everyone else. Al Dean calls him a tiger. He's that all right. He'll get what he wants." Clearly, "Tiger" was an apt tag for him. He moves gracefully and has the killer instinct. Sitting on a motel bed in snappy sports clothes, he is all deceptive charm. Sitting on a pit wall in coveralls, his eyes and thoughts hidden behind sunglasses, he is calm and cool. Sitting in the cockpit of a racing car, he is what he really is, all race driver, daring in a deadly profession.

5. The
Rich
Man

WITH Andretti's meteoric rise to prominence came responsibilities and the opportunities to make side money which began to distract him from racing, and which tested the new champion's dedication. Everyone wanted a piece of him, especially after he conducted himself publicly with class. Interviewers besieged him, but he gave everyone time and spoke openly to them. He wasn't hung up on it, but he did it. When Chuck Barnes could not arrange a television taping at a reasonable hour, Andretti arose at 4:30 one morning to do it.

Early in the season, writer Barbara La Fontaine of *Sports Illustrated* pursued him into Ohio, where he was hustling on a series of personal appearances, and a story she tells about the troubles he had with his tour manager, whom she called Harry because Harry was not his name, was most revealing. As the week wore on, and the schedule got hotter and tighter, Harry began to drink. By Friday with Mario due to drive back to Indianapolis, Harry was missing with Mario's car, his driving suit, and his helmet, and Mario had alerted friends to look for him and had been searching for him through the day, narrowly missing him a couple of times.

Telephoning around, Mario finally reached Harry who gave him directions to the car in a distant part of Dayton. Mario rented a car and drove off in search of his car. When he got where Harry said the car would be, there was no car. He drove around other places, but still no car. Finally, he returned to the hotel where the desk clerk informed him that if he was looking for his friend, he was up on the ninth floor trying to get in the wrong room. Mario charged up to the ninth floor, found Harry in a room on a bed and asked him where the car was. Harry said it was right downstairs in the parking lot.

Mario charged down to the parking lot,

searched for the car, failed to find it, and charged back up to the ninth floor again. Harry had passed out. Mario looked for a bucket of water to throw on him, finally settled for a glass of water. Harry came to and asked Mario what the heck he was doing, had he been drinking? Mario rather unhappily pointed out it was Harry, not Mario, who had been drinking. Harry asked sadly if Mario was mad at him. Mario asked him if he knew where the car was. We'll find the car, Harry said, don't you worry, we'll find the car.

Mario threw a coat on Harry and took him down to his rented car and Harry directed Mario to a street in another neighborhood where he pointed at a car and said, triumphantly, "There it is." It was a blue Mercury. Mario's car was a tan station wagon. Informed of his error, Harry was deeply disappointed. Then he realized he was in front of a friend's house and suggested the friend might know where the car was. They went to see the friend who said that he had often gone out to look for Harry's cars and often found them, and would be glad to go out with them to look for this one.

They drove off and looked in many places without finding the car. At one point, the friend commented to Mario, "You drive better than I do. But then you got a better car." Mario did not comment on this. Finally, in a parking lot across from the newspaper office where Harry had many friends, the car was spotted and everyone descended on it with cries of triumph. By this time, it was dark. Without reprimanding Harry or ever once having spoken harshly to him, Mario bid him farewell and drove off through the night toward his destination.

He simply had to endure such moments as his life became hectic. He signed a lucrative contract to represent Firestone and drive on its tires, and later an equally lucrative contract to represent Ford, to use Ford engines and to drive Ford cars in such races as were possible. He signed with two dozen different sponsors, whose decals began to grace his cars. Because racing drivers can represent a wider variety of products reasonably—from cars to engines, from tires to gasoline, from shock absorbers to spark plugs, and so forth—than can athletes in any other sport, they are more attractive to more wealthy firms. The result is that race drivers can make more money than any other sports figures. Not only can they win a lot of money on the track, but can earn a lot of side money.

According to Chuck Barnes, Mario suddenly vaulted into an exclusive group which included also Foyt, Jones, Gurney, and a few southern stock-car standouts, such as Richard Petty, who were guaranteed $250,000 before they even turned a wheel, before they even won a race that year. If they did not keep winning, they would not continue to command such sums, of course, but a quarter of a million dollars is sufficient reason for a driver to permit himself to be distracted from racing. Mario conceded, "Suddenly I'm making more money than I ever dreamed existed in the world." Jones warned, however, "It begins to get very dangerous for a top driver when the pressures of outside problems and commitments distract him from his profession and prevent him from spending the time to prepare his car and practice for each race properly, as he did on the way up."

Aware of this, Mario virtually stopped going home so he could devote a proper amount of time to racing, while still spending time on his outside interests. He took his family with him whenever possible and became more than ever a gypsy, travelling the tour from town to town, living out of a suitcase on the road, spending long hours getting from one place to the next, and long hours in hotel and motel rooms and his trailer.

His year, 1966, started in sadness. Driving a Ferrari sports car at the Twelve Hours of Sebring endurance race in Florida early in the year, Mario's gears locked and he spun, bumping Don Wester's Porsche into a small group of persons who were watching the race from an area forbidden to spectators. Four were killed. Having continued on, Mario was unaware of the tragedy for awhile. He went into the pits to inspect the damage on his car, which promptly burst into flames. Mario escaped unburnt and it was only after the fire had been extinguished that he learned of the disaster. He slumped sadly, head hung as though he was going to be sick.

Later, he was able to accept it. "It was just one of those things," he said. "The accident was racing luck. Those people should not have been where they were, or should not have been permitted there. It depresses me, but I'll go on. This is what I do."

Mario had two cars for the championship circuit and Indy, a Hawk revamped by Brawner and McGee and a Lotus-Ford ordered from England. He preferred the trusty old Hawk. At Phoenix, in the season inaugural, a 150-miler, he sped around the mile in 29.49 seconds in qualifying, the first ever to break the thirty-second barrier on a mile oval, and set a new mile-oval world record at 122 miles per hour.

The race was rough. From the first, Andretti and Foyt duelled out front. On the 104th lap, Foyt tried to pass Andretti on the inside and they went through the backstretch side by side with neither giving ground as they turned into the corner. They slipped inside a slower car, side by side, but, cramped, made contact and locked, spinning into the infield in a haze of dust.

Both got going again, but Andretti's car then

quit within two laps, Foyt's within four. Jim McElreath won. Afterwards, one of the Dean crew was complaining that Foyt had drifted into his man's side, when Mario spoke sharply. "We were both racing hard. Don't blame anybody," he said.

At Trenton, Mario qualified in a course-record 115 miles per hour. In the race, he led from the start until the eighteenth lap, when Foyt crept past him. Foyt led for twenty-two laps with Andretti hanging to his tail, then was blown down by Mario on the fortieth lap, smoothly and surely, and left far back. Foyt retired at eighty-five laps with his gears shot. At this point, Andretti led Ward by twenty-five seconds, but he ran over a piece of metal that had dropped off another car, slashed a tire, and had to pit to replace it, as Ward rolled into the lead.

Mario returned far back, but was in fourth place and closing ground on the leaders when rain began to fall and the race was halted after 102 laps. He might well have won had the race gone the forty-eight more laps to its finish, but that's racing luck and all Mario could do was shrug it off. This was the forty-five-year-old Ward's first championship victory in more than two years, and the twenty-sixth and, as it was to turn out, the last of the veteran's grand career.

As Ward accepted congratulation in victory

row, Andretti stood, grease-smeared and disappointed, but straight and patient, signing autographs and telling everyone who asked that he felt fine, which was not true, but which was his way.

Andretti was coolly confident. He felt ready to win the big one at Indianapolis in his second try at it, especially after the first two weeks of practice when he ran much faster than his competitors. Over the winter, he had turned in an unofficial record lap of more than 164 m.p.h. while testing tires there. Now he ran the unofficial record to 168 m.p.h. As the opening of time-trials neared, he became a heavy favorite to win the pole position.

Ward was first out and averaged 159, which was ordinary, but which he guessed would get him into the starting field and so satisfied him. Then, Mario went out. The perfection of his performance is best reflected by the consistency of his clockings. He turned the first two-and-one-half-mile lap in 54.11 seconds, the second in 54.18, the third in 54.25, and the fourth in 54.46. Only three-tenths of a second, less than a man can count, separated one lap from another. This translated into speeds of 166.328 miles per hour, 166.112, 165.899, and 165.259. The first lap was a new one-lap record, as was the average for ten miles of 165.899.

He was disappointed. "I had been practicing faster. I was going faster on the second lap when I almost lost it in a turn and that may have caused my foot to lift just a touch. That's all it takes." He shrugged and smiled. "I'm happy to get the records, but I don't think it'll last any longer than the ones I set last year. I'd love to have the pole, but the other guys are waiting for me. Maybe some of 'em can catch me."

They couldn't. Clark came closest at 164.144. Young George Snider, driving for A. J. Foyt's team, filled the front row at 162.5. Jones, Ruby, and Johncock filled the second row. Ward and Briton Graham Hill landed in the fifth row. Foyt crashed and worked overnight to repair his car. He made it on the second day in the sixth row. Gurney landed in the seventh row.

Chuck Rodee slid during his trial run. His car reversed itself and backed into the wall with such force that the car's metal starter shaft was driven five inches into the concrete. Rodee was rushed to the hospital, where he died.

Race day. Andretti drove to the airport where a helicopter was supposed to pick him up to fly him to the Speedway, dropping him in the infield and saving him from the enormous crush of crowd and traffic working its way through the streets to the arena. The helicopter did not show up. Andretti called up his garage and Jim McGee hopped on a motorcycle and drove through the crush to the airport, picked up Andretti, and drove him back through the crush to the track. "Just like Laurel and Hardy," Andretti said later.

They were on time. The tension built through the pre-race festivities. The music, the bombs, the balloons. "Gentlemen, start your engines." They did and the cars moved away. As Andretti took the green flag and led the field into the first turn, hell erupted behind him. Billy Foster, trying to gain ground along the wall from the fourth row, brushed the wall, slid into Gordon Johncock's car, and touched off a massive melee. "Oh my God, not now, not already," Arnie Knepper said in his cockpit as, seconds from the start, cars were crashing into each other. Their wheels were breaking off and bouncing around, and metal was raining into the stands. It was a madhouse of smoke and sparks and the sounds of bending metal and screaming fans, as the cars careened to a stop.

Sixteen cars were involved in the accident and eleven were damaged too badly to continue. These included the cars of Foster, Foyt and Gurney. Foyt had ground to a halt at the end of the mainstretch, jumped from his car, and climbed a fence for safety. "What a damn stupid waste," he said later. Gurney said, "Each driver has an accelerator and a brake. It's too bad they don't all have brains, too." Incredibly, though, while hundreds of thousands of dollars worth of equipment was ruined and a lot of time and effort preparing for the race thrown into discard, no one was seriously hurt. Fourteen fans did have to be treated for minor injuries from debris landing in the stands.

After the second stoppage in three years, the race resumed with Andretti leading the twenty-two remaining cars through several slow warmup laps. He said later that as he got the green to return to speed and pressed down on the accelerator, he knew something was wrong. "It was just like putting my foot in a tub of Jello," he said. The engine responded roughly. These delicate machines are built to be run fast, not started and stopped and started again and run slowly for a long time. Andretti's valves were fouled up. Soon, his engine began to sputter and he slowed. He made a quick stop to change spark plugs, but then at sixty-seven miles, he coasted into the pits and parked his sick car and got out of it and stood looking at it as though he could not believe it had betrayed him. Brawner poked around in the guts of the engine, then turned away in disgust. Dean tilted his head back and stared silently at the heavens. Andretti got out and sat on the ground by the pit wall with his head hung between his knees and stared silently at the ground.

As the race wore on, car after car went bad. Ward pulled into the pits at 185 miles saying his car wasn't good enough and there was no point proceeding further. At this point, Clark,

Jones, and Ruby were running one-two-three. Clark's mishandling car spun out, but he kept going and held the lead. No driver had ever spun out and continued on to win the 500. A bit later, Clark spun out and kept going again, but this time he lost the lead. Several cars passed him. Ruby took the lead followed by Scot Jackie Stewart.

At 365 miles, Ruby led by fifty seconds, but began to throw oil heavily and was black-flagged into the pits, beaten. Then Stewart led. But at 480 miles, leading by fifty-five seconds, Stewart's car used up the last of its oil and was coasted to a stop in the infield. Suddenly, Hill, who never had contended for the lead, led, with Clark second. Hill took the checkered flag and coasted into Victory Lane. Clark came across and coasted toward Victory Lane, too, thinking Hill never had passed him. Stopped, Clark and his sponsor, Andy Granatelli, argued with officials, but were denied. Later, a recheck of scoring records supported the officials.

Hill, a suave Briton who looks like actor David Niven, waved happily to the crowd. The Dairy Council pays winners who drink milk to toast their victory five hundred dollars. As the television cameras ground away, Hill was handed the traditional bottle of milk, drank thirstily from it, then made a disgusted face and thrust it away from him. Then the race queen, a young beauty, bent to give the winner the traditional kiss. Hill kissed her briefly, politely. Then he took a long look at her, considered their brief romance, and pulled her to him and kissed her hard and long as the crowd roared.

At the Victory Dinner, Ward retired tearfully. Hill, the second straight Grand Prix driver to win American's classic racing event, collected $156,297 for his team. Clark collected $76,992. Andretti placed eighteenth, picking up $25,120.

"I'll get over it. In a hundred years or so," he said. "I'm disappointed," he conceded. "There's still a long season to go, though, and I still hope to retain my national title."

With another winner taking his 1,000 points back to Europe, the contest was wide open. And in the Milwaukee 100, Mario jumped right into the thick of it. Before 37,000 fans, Andretti set a track record of 111 m.p.h. in qualifications and led from start to finish to win, picking up $11,477 of the $41,060 purse. It had not been an easy race. After one hour and two minutes of running, Andretti had squeezed the steering wheel so tightly that when he went to lift his hands off the wheel to wave to the crowd, his muscles would not respond and his hands would not move.

Foyt had been burned in a practice crash and Ruby in the crash of a light airplane, softening

Andretti's task. "I missed them," Mario said, grinning.

In the Langhorne 100, Mario set a new world record for a paved mile with a 122.615 m.p.h. trial, then again led wire to wire to win, holding off McElreath at the wire. In the Atlanta 300, Andretti won the pole position for the third straight race with a record of 169.014 m.p.h. for the one-and-one-half-mile banked oval, then led wire to wire to win by four laps, becoming the first driver in USAC history to lead all of three consecutive races and for five hundred consecutive miles. Foyt returned to action in this one, but his blistered hands curtailed his effort at five laps. No one was talking about cheap titles now. Headed for his second straight championship, Andretti was winning regularly.

In the Hoosier Grand Prix road race, Andretti was nosed out in qualifying by Ruby. He grabbed the lead at the start, but then spun out and lost the lead for the first time in a month of races. Rolling into the pits to be checked out, Andretti was ready to retire for the day, but Brawner urged him to keep going. Andretti did. He faced an imposing task, having fallen two laps behind. He had to pass twenty-nine cars twice to retain the lead. Relentlessly, he cut down the cars in front of him. Lap after lap, he picked off cars and picked up ground.

Some of the leaders began to break down in front of him. Andretti lapped everyone once, twice, regained the lead with thirty-eight laps to go and won his fourth consecutive title event going away.

It was perhaps his greatest driving feat and afterwards he praised Brawner for goading him to continue. Shaking his head with wonder, Andretti said, "I can't believe it. I just can't believe it."

His victory streak ended at Langhorne. Mario upped the world record for a mile to 123.839 m.p.h. on his first qualifying lap, but spun and crashed into the wall on his second lap. He was not hurt, but was eliminated. Determined to run, he jumped into another car, hurried into the time trials without even warming up, qualified twentieth, started there, passed ten cars in the first five laps and had advanced into seventh place when he began to blow oil all over the oval at thirty-three laps and had to quit.

In the Milwaukee 200, Mario won the pole at 111.4 and the race at 104.0, his fifth of the season, battling Johncock bitterly, losing and regaining the lead twice before prevailing. It was a cruelly hot day and after receiving the victory trophy and a check for $14,548, Mario passed out from heat prostration and exhaustion. Revived, he grinned with embarrassment and insisted he was fine.

On to the Springfield 100. Here, Andretti fought Foyt wheel to wheel for ninety-two miles before his tire began to shred and he had to drop back. Then Foyt began to run out of fuel and he also had to drop back. Don Branson went on to win. In the DuQuoin 100, Andretti's engine exploded in qualifying and he watched from the pit wall. The other favorites also broke down as the race progressed and Bud Tingelstad scored an upset triumph.

Springfield and DuQuoin were dirt races. So was the Hoosier Hundred, next up. This was the most traditional form of American racing, but since the arrival of the fragile rear-engine lightweights, many dirt tracks were being paved over and the number of dirt races on the title tour was declining sharply and were threatened with elimination entirely. Many old hands mourned this turn of events. Many felt dirt racing was a truer test of a driver than paved racing. On rough dirt, the cars bounced around severely and were broadslid wildly through the turns, kicking up rooster-tails of dust. They had to be manhandled. The brawny Foyt was the master of this form of racing. The tiny Andretti had yet to win a dirt race on the title trail and many felt he would not, citing this as a weakness which demeaned him as a true champion.

Andretti, who had almost won the Spring-field 100, came through to win the Hoosier

Hundred. He was lucky to win, trailing Foyt for ninety-seven miles and passing him to win when Foyt's brake pedal broke as he headed into a turn and he bounced off the wall and out of the lead. "It's a great thrill winning, anyway," Andretti said later. "This is a classic dirt test. I won't say I like dirt racing as much as paved racing. It's rough and you spit out dirt for days, but coming up I won more than my share on dirt tracks and I think I've proved I can handle them."

Brawner said, "There aren't as many big dirt races as there used to be. Guys like Foyt had more opportunity to learn on dirt. They're more comfortable on it than Andretti is. Guys like Foyt who are bigger and physically stronger might be better suited to it, but I have to think that given the same amount of experience on dirt, Andretti would hold his own with anyone. I can't imagine the kind of racing in which Andretti would be outclassed for long."

On the dirt at Sacramento, young Dick Atkins won. Then, in a sprint-car race on the dirt at Ascot Park near Los Angeles, young Atkins and old Don Branson crashed and were killed.

The trail wound to a halt on the mile at Phoenix with the two-hundred-mile Bobby Ball Memorial Classic. It was the fifteenth and last race on the circuit. Andretti already had clinched the crown. He arrived early and sat in the southwestern sun on this November day and watched as Brawner and McGee and Tony Buffone and the rest of the Dean crew readied the car. Then he lowered himself into the cockpit of his car, enclosed in fiberglass, his rump only inches above the ground, and careened around the course in 28.31 seconds, raising his own record for the course to 123 m.p.h.

As the race began, Andretti got out of the turn first and took the lead. On the second lap, Art Pollard lost control of his car and spun. Trying to avoid him, Bud Tingelstad spun his car and was hit by Ralph Liguori's car, which flipped end over end in front of the horrified grandstand spectators before settling to a stop in a tangle of twisted metal. Somehow, none of the drivers were hurt. Andretti and the remainder of the field picked through the mess.

Foyt went out on the forty-seventh mile when his rear suspension failed. Andretti was not pressed until the eighty-fifth lap, then Jones caught him and passed him. For the next forty-eight miles, Andretti hung on Jones's tail, applying pressure to the veteran. At the 128th mile, Andretti pressed past Jones. Jones's car was worn out by the lengthy duel. Within a lap, his brakes were gone, a rod snapped in his engine, his car hurtled out of control into a wall, teetering momentarily on two wheels, threatening to flip, then settling back to a stop in an upright position. As Jones scrambled safely from the car, it exploded in flames.

The rest of the way, it was all Andretti, monotonously Mario lap after smooth lap. After one hour, fifty-four minutes and fifty-eight seconds, he swept across the finish line under the checkered flag and coasted into Victory Lane to the cheers of the crowd. He had averaged 104 m.p.h. and earned his team $8,709. He pushed himself out of the cockpit and perched, weary and sweaty, on the rear roll bar, his feet in the seat. A bottle of champagne was thrust into his hands and he put his parched lips to it and drank from it. He wiped his face with his hands, leaving a smear of grease on his cheeks.

This, except for a one-shot side-trip to Japan for the Fuji 200—an experimental event, which Jackie Stewart won after Andretti blew an engine in practice—concluded the campaign. Early in the season Mario had signed a contract with Montgomery Ward for five hundred dollars every time he made a brief appearance at one of the chain's stores. He had collected exactly once. He had nothing against money, but he simply was unwilling to undersell races to make side money.

He raced in all kinds of cars all year. He won the one-hundred-lap, fifty-mile Pat O'Connor–Joe James Memorial sprint-car race at Salem, Indiana, for the second time and he won a one-hundred-lap midget-car feature at Oswego, New York, for the first time, which he would later, the following season, win again. He shared a ride with Pedro Rodriguez of Mexico in a Ferrari in the Daytona Continental, finishing fourth, and had that deadly experience in a Ferrari at Sebring.

On the championship trail, he drove all fifteen races, and was the fastest qualifier in nine, including seven straight, and set one-lap records at all six of USAC's major paved ovals, including the world records for one-mile and one-and-one-half-mile tracks and the Indianapolis record for that two-and-one-half-mile track. He won eight events, including four in a row, and an unprecedented three in a row wire to wire. He had successfully defended his national driving championship, becoming the sixth driver in the sixty-five-year history of the contest to win it twice in a row. No one was criticizing him as a "cheese champion" now.

Not all the purses were big, but they added up. For the second straight year, Mario earned close to six figures in USAC racing alone, picking up $95,701. His life had altered. He was totally committed to racing and established as one of the dominant drivers. Only his failure to win at Indianapolis detracted from his stature, but he had plenty of time for that.

6. The Frustrated One

IT WAS a December morning in Indiana, grey, cold, the streets flecked with remnants of a previous snow. At the Indianapolis Motor Speedway, a small white car, seeming smaller than usual in the vastness of the otherwise deserted track, was alone and going fast. The sound of the car's whining engine cut eerily through the still air.

In the pits, tire specialists and engineers and the car's crew checked the electric timer and kept a keen eye on the car as it hurried around. Alongside the pits, the attendants who run the fire trucks and ambulances and other emergency vehicles, which must be readied whenever cars are run, watched intently.

This was tire-testing time, six months before the next 500. In this case, Firestone was testing its new racing tires for the coming classic and the other races on the championship trail. Later on, Goodyear would test its new tires. Firestone had dominated the trail and the 500 for many years, but when Goodyear joined the battle in the 1960's, competition between the two became intense.

Most drivers will tell you it is improvement in tires—smaller, wider tires which grip the road better—which more than anything else is responsible for the improvement in speed. Tires have been developed for Indy cars which simply do not blow out within 500 miles unless punctured, and which do not have to be replaced in 500 miles.

In December, the new, improved cars and engines which will run in the spring and summer, at Indianapolis and into the fall, are not ready and will have to be tested later, possibly in March or April at Phoenix, or in May at Indianapolis when the race is near and time is short. But the new tires are ready, or being readied now, and Andretti, a valuable member of the Firestone team, is testing them.

As he is flagged into the pits, he pulls in and shuts off, shivering in the chill, and watches as the engineers stick temperature-gauge needles into the tires to get heat readings. Others confer with Andretti to get his impressions. "Unlike many drivers, he can tell you what is happening out there," a Firestone executive says. "He is a real pro," says Ford racing boss Jacque Passino.

Wherever he goes, he is pursued by reporters. Leo Levine, preparing a piece for *True* Magazine, is observing now, later to lay out this scene. Andretti is waved out and swiftly accelerates to speed.

He comes around and down the mainstretch past the pits, right-side tires two feet from the wall, then dives hard into the corner, cutting across it to the inside line, braking at the last possible moment to permit him to negotiate it, then accelerating again at the first possible moment to use the short stretch at speed as much as possible, then braking down through the second turn, then accelerating out of it into the backstretch, driven by centrifugal force to the outer wall, then braking through the third turn, accelerating into the second short stretch, then braking through the fourth turn, accelerating into the homestretch and through it.

"The straights are simple," Andretti says. "You go through them as fast as you can. The secret of high speeds is going into the corner as fast as you can stand it and staying in the ballpark. You pick up the throttle slightly before you enter the corner. Then the drift starts. It is very important how you enter the corner. Usually, you have a spot you aim for. And if you miss, as sometimes happens, let me tell you it can be very thrilling.

"Coming out of the corner it is important to apply the throttle—hard—and pick a spot on the wall on the short chute to drift to. You no sooner are in the short chute, then you have to start thinking of the approach to the next turn. The timing has to be close to perfect. You can't be too late or too early. A slight miscue costs you precious seconds. Then you are on the backstretch, going as fast as you can, with nothing to worry about but two more turns. And every turn is slightly different."

Andretti corners the quarter-mile turns at Indianapolis in six seconds or less. He gets through the short straights in three seconds or less. He gets through the long straights in twelve seconds or less. He reaches a peak of more than 150 miles per hour through the corners and accelerates up to 180, 200, 215 miles per hour at the middle of the long stretches. At these speeds, the world is a dizzying blur. Every bump, every slip, every rough spot in the road is magnified. "That's why you practice," Andretti says. "To recognize every inch of the road. When you hit something and your car does something, it doesn't bother you because you know what to expect from it."

In traffic, it is something else. It is not as easy to pick the places you want to be on the track because another car may be in some of those places. "You come off a turn and see another car. Almost as soon as you see him—boom —he's right in front of you," Andretti says. "You have to judge immediately how fast he is going and make up your mind the moment you see him what you are going to do." To pass or not to pass? When and where?

"You also must figure the possibility that he does not know you are there and might drift up on you just as you start to pass," Andretti points out. "So you try to get alongside him in a turn so he will know you are there. Then, there usually is no problem. But if you make one miscalculation on your speed or his, you'll have to make a last-second correction, and chances are it will throw you out of control."

At speeds of above 150 mile per hour, on a hard surface which may be slick with oil, a car will skid hundreds of yards before the driver can even begin to attempt to control it. These cars are travelling one hundred yards every second. Count one. That is one hundred yards. Whap!

"Then there is the hair-raising possibility," Andretti points out, "that you suddenly will come upon a car that is spinning or going backwards. In this case, all I can say is he who hesitates is lost. You make up your mind—one way or another—what to do. Then you do it. You can't hesitate for a fraction of a second." Usually, race drivers point for an accident, feeling it is moving and will be somewhere else by the time they get there. But if a car is going to bounce off a wall, you have to judge that, too.

"Fans would be surprised," says Andretti, "how many times we scare ourselves on a race track. A driver will come in and say, 'I was real sloppy,' or 'I lost it in every turn.' The fans noticed nothing, but the driver may have had a few seconds when only experienced and conditioned reflexes saved him from a slide."

Which is why, for one dollar a mile, Andretti and Foyt and Jones and the lucky ones who can land the assignments drive tire tests at Indianapolis and elsewhere, but mostly at Indianapolis, because the more they get to know the track on lonely, cold December mornings, when they are alone, the more split-seconds they can find hiding in corners there, the better they can qualify and race in traffic on crowded, hot May afternoons.

The stakes are highest at Indianapolis, so the practice is most intense there, but the winners practice everywhere they race. They walk the courses on the morning of races to see how the surface is that day and what the weather is like and what the wind is like, because there are places on racing tracks where gusting winds pick up a light car racing fast and toss it around.

Mario is an individualist, a perfectionist, with a very businesslike nature. He totes a brief case to every track and after every practice session and after every race he writes about it in a big notebook. "I've always done this," he told Ray Marquette of *The Indianapolis Star* and *The Sporting News.* "Every time I run a track, I write down gear setups that haven't worked, tire setups, chassis adjustments and my running speeds."

He tries everything in practice because he can experiment in practice, running in different places on the track, seeking different "grooves," trying to take the turns different ways, taking chances, which he could not bother with or would not dare in qualifying and in race traffic.

He writes down weather conditions and track conditions, and then when he gets to a track in a certain car for a certain race on a given day, he can check his book to see what worked and didn't work under similar circumstances before, and consult with his crew and try to set up for the race intelligently and scientifically.

Andretti watches what others do and listens to what others say, but he goes his own way and finds his own way. He has his own style and he likes to set up cars his way, and what works best for him might not work best for Foyt, for example. It is a very complicated business, not just pressing on the accelerator and steering and hanging on. There is that, too, and if you are not one of the good ones, it doesn't matter how scientifically you prepare, you are not going to win. But everyone can improve his racing, and if you are an Andretti, you seek every edge you can find to help you win over a Foyt or a Jones or a Gurney.

Some don't write these things down, but they feel them or file them in their minds. Andretti is one of the meticulous ones who writes things down and doesn't trust to memory. "If you can't show it to me in black and white, I'm not interested," he says. He makes up his own mind about things and forms rigid opinions and he is not easily swayed from these. Some say he never changes his mind about things. Yet he isn't really stubborn.

Clint Brawner said, "He makes suggestions and he listens to suggestions. He has an open mind about things. A driver can let a mechanic do it all or he can help him or he can try to do it all himself. Foyt tries to do it all. Andretti helps. Sachs lets the mechanic do it all." Jim McGee said, "Mario is much more knowing about cars than most drivers. He understands cars and can explain what is happening to them at speed and can help us to rig the chassis the way he can do best with it."

Yet, none of this would have been of great value if Andretti did not have a natural instinct for his trade. Al Dean pointed out, "I notice sometimes Brawner and Andretti don't talk to each other while working on a car. The car talks to them and they understand it and each other." Rodger Ward said, "Andretti has a 'feel' for this thing. No matter how well you plan, situations develop in races which are unexpected, and you must improvise to meet them. Of course, experience plays a big part in your reacting swiftly, almost by reflex, and correctly to each situation as it unfolds. Andretti seems able to 'feel' his way through situations."

"Some drivers," said Brawner, "are good in tests, some are good in practice, some are good in qualifying, some are good in racing. Very few are good in everything. Mario is. Some drivers are great qualifiers. This is very important. You save a lot by starting up front and it gives you the best chance to win. But if you're no good in traffic, it doesn't matter, you'll get passed and drop back. Some drivers couldn't care less about practicing or qualifying, they need competition to challenge them, and when they get in traffic, they're tough.

"Sachs was no good testing or practicing, but he was a great qualifier and a fine competitor. Bryan couldn't have cared less about anything but racing. He was a terrible qualifier. He penalized himself by getting terrible starting positions. But he was so great in traffic, in competition, that he usually made up for it. He went the hard way, but he got there.

"Most of the great ones, like Foyt and Jones and Gurney and Andretti, are good at everything. Foyt can't stand for anyone to be ahead of him in anything. Andretti is much the same way. He's not vain, really. Publicly, he's very modest. But, inside of himself, he does think he's the best, and he always wants to prove it. I don't think anyone could be the best if he didn't think he was the best. I'm sure A. J. thinks he's the best. I'm sure Parnelli does. I'm sure Dan does. And I know Mario does. And, you know something, Mario isn't far from proving his point."

Mario Andretti began 1967 by taking on the best of the southern stock-car drivers on their home grounds, the high-banked, super-fast, two-and-one-half-mile Daytona International Raceway, and beating them in their "Indy," the Daytona 500, which launches them on their trail each season. His victory there was a tremendous upset and added immensely to his prestige and bankroll.

Then he shifted into a Ford sports car and, alternating with Bruce McLaren, drove 1,237 miles through daylight and darkness to beat the standout sports-car chauffeurs in the gruelling "Twelve Hour Grand Prix of Endurance" at Sebring, Florida, where he had participated in the fatal accident a year earlier.

Jacque Passino of Ford pointed out that in

testing at Kingman, Arizona, Andretti told them their sports car would run faster if they removed an experimental "spoiler" they had hung on the sides and back, and he was right. At Sebring, he realized the car was "bottoming," scraping the track although the track was fairly flat, which turned out to be correct, and enabled them to hike it up and save time and damage; and at Daytona, he suggested some sway bar changes that gave the stock car much increased stability.

On the heels of his two tremendous and prestigious triumphs at Daytona and Sebring, Mario returned to championship cars and the championship circuit near the peak of his profession, but without the confidence one might have expected. He had a new and powerful rear-engine lightweight built for him by Brawner and McGee, who became co-chief mechanics this year, and he had confidence in this car, but he was concerned about a turbine car that had been developed by Andy Granatelli and would be driven by Parnelli Jones in the 500.

The word was out that this experimental car was more of a jet plane than a race car, could run faster, longer and more reliably than piston-driven cars on big tracks, and in the hands of a peerless performer like Parnelli might be impossible to top.

As the fraternity convened at Phoenix for

the first championship race of the season, Mario mourned, "I have to wonder if I'll ever be as far ahead of the field at Indy as I was last year. I had much the best car, was able to qualify much the fastest, and could have outrun everyone easily if my valves hadn't fouled up. This doesn't mean I can't win that race yet, but it does mean I may never again have as good a chance to win."

The turbine was still only a rumor at Phoenix, but troubles developed swiftly for Andretti anyway. In warmups the day before the race, he slammed his car into a wall, demolished it and shook himself up severely. The Belgian driver Lucien Bianchi loaned him a car and Andretti threw a wheel while qualifying it on race day and put it into a wall, damaging it severely and shaking himself up further. He was a spectator as Lloyd Ruby won the race, the Jimmy Bryan Memorial 150, from start to finish.

Mario had his car rebuilt and it was finished late the following week and towed to Trenton and rolled off the trailer minutes before warmups for the 150-miler there. Mario hopped in it, was first out to qualify and promptly set a new track record of 116.4 m.p.h. From the pole, he shot into the lead on the first lap of the race and was never headed. He averaged 109 and won handily.

As he pointed the nose of his car into the

victory circle, the number one lettered boldly across the nose, proud symbol of his reign as U. S. champion, he grinned with relief, and as he stopped and was interviewed, he said, "I'm most happy for my mechanics, who worked so hard to put this thing back together again after my accident at Phoenix, and did it so well it behaved beautifully all the way."

The turbine waited at Indianapolis. Andy Granatelli had competed at Indianapolis and on the championship trail as driver, mechanic, sponsor and car owner for twenty-one years without winning a single race. He had crashed at Indy and been badly hurt there. He had, with his brothers, built an engineering business and returned to Indy, backing cars without success. He had developed STP fuel additive, sold it and himself to the Studebaker Corporation, and publicized it and himself to enormous success. He had become a millionaire and spent much of it backing Indy cars, such as Novi cars, which not only didn't win the race, but seldom finished it and sometimes didn't even make it.

Granatelli was an individualist. He wanted to do things others didn't do. He wanted to win Indy on his own terms. The Novi was the most powerful engine ever devised for Indy. All racing cars which used various Novi engines, altered over the years, came to be called Novis, great crowd favorites. But the Novi engine never was harnessed successfully and always failed, if sometimes dramatically. Granatelli bought rights to the Novi and ran it to failure through the middle 1960's, when he shifted to a turbine. He had spent $600,000 to develop a turbine racing car which was permissible under existing Indianapolis rules and by 1967 he was ready with it and had signed Parnelli, who had won the pole at Indianapolis twice and the race once, to drive it.

Although Granatelli's rotund figure had been made familiar through television commercials and he had become something close to a folk hero with the general public, he was disliked and ridiculed by many at Indy. Jones said, "A lot of guys laugh at Andy. They resent him because he's a very dominating type of guy. A lot of people want to be against whatever Andy's for." But Jones and others figured Granatelli was a very sound businessman and a sharp operator who had so far failed on the championship trail with radical experiments, but inevitably would come up with something better than anyone else had, and the turbine was it. Granatelli, himself, said. "The powers-that-be at Indy are scared of this car. They don't like anything too different from the norm. And if it wins here, they'll find a way to ban it or legislate it out of existence, you just watch."

Observing it in practice, many wanted to ban it. It ran silently, so others never were sure where it was. Its exhaust belched back shimmering heat waves. Foyt complained, "This is a proving ground for cars, not jet planes." Andretti said, "It's out of our class." Owner J. C. Agajanian said, "If this thing is as good as we think it is, we all may have to junk an awful lot of expensive equipment." Most seemed sure the car was being run under wraps and was far superior to the field.

It was superior on the turns, which is critical, but not on the straightaways. Jones had discovered this and other factors, though he would not confess them publicly. It was a difficult car to drive. Unlike most racing engines, the turbine did not respond instantly to acceleration. And once wound up, it did not unwind easily, so the braking did not take hold instantly. And it was hard on the brakes. Parnelli was a master and he could handle these time lags and other problems, especially with an advantage cornering. However, he knew also that the engine was delicate and as he ran faster than 167 or 168 miles per hour the gears began to give way.

On the opening day of time trials, Jones took the turbine out early and qualified it carefully at 166.075 with two laps in the 165 range and two in the 166 range. This was slower than most had expected and encouraged Andretti that he might be able to capture the coveted pole position again. He did. Five cars ran faster than Jones's turbine—those of Andretti, Gurney, Johncock, Foyt, and Leonard, in that order. Andretti flew flawlessly through laps of 53.19, 53.25, 53.01 and 53.59 seconds, which convert to clockings of 169.205, 169.014, 169.779 and 167.942 miles per hour and gave him an average of 168.982. His fastest lap and average again were new records. And he was the fifth driver in history to win the pole twice in a row.

He steamed into the pits to the applause of the people and Dean said, "Did you see that little Eyetalian go! Oh, my, this is our year at last." But Andretti was not so sure. He had hoped to penetrate the 170 mile-per-hour barrier. "I was trying to get through the corners without using my brakes. I made it on a couple of corners, but on that last lap I almost lost it in a corner and gave myself a thrill. That's as fast as I can go."

He remained unconvinced that Jones in the turbine would not be too much for him on race day. "All I can do, all any of us can do," Andretti said, "is run as hard as we can and try to keep enough pressure on him so maybe he'll use up his brakes or something will bust on his car." Gurney said, "He can run faster than we can. I don't know if he can run longer."

On race day, it was cool and cloudy. It looked like rain, but few felt it would. The 500 is famous for good luck in weather. It may rain for days before or days afterward, but seldom on Memorial Day. It may rain on the morning or the evening of Memorial Day, but never the afternoon. Or at least it had not rained sufficiently to curtail a race for more than twenty-five years, though, as the song suggests, it does rain in Indianapolis in the summertime.

The green flag flew and the cars blasted into the first turn. Safely, unlike the year before, Andretti came off the pole into the lead. Suddenly, however, between the first and second turns, Jones's turbocar swept around five cars in front of him and into the lead. The crowd came up screaming. It had been a swift and easy and devastating move. Later, Andretti mourned, "I looked up and he was by me. The son of a gun didn't even have the decency to wave."

It didn't matter, not to Andretti. Almost as soon as he accelerated to top speed, his clutch began to come apart. He could not believe it. He sat in his car, which had been so carefully built and so finely prepared by master mechanics and which had run so beautifully in qualifying, and he couldn't believe that in the first few laps of the world's richest race it was falling apart around him, much as his car had the previous year, only sooner.

He turned into the pits and shouted at Brawner who tried something and sent him out again. It was no good, and he turned into the pits again and shouted at Brawner, who threw up the hood disgustedly and began to search around inside.

The cars kept running until the black clouds broke and the rain came down. At eighteen laps, Jones was far in front and pulling away, but the race had to be stopped. Officials waited most of the day, but the rain did not stop. The race was postponed to be resumed the next day. The last of the great crowd worked its way out. It was a break for the Dean team, which could put in a new clutch overnight, but what was the use? Six laps behind, Mario no longer had any chance to win. He would run, but hopelessly.

He said, "You have to condition yourself to defeat, to frustration, you have to learn to accept it. . . . Racing has to be the most unpredictable sport in the world. So many little things can happen. I never, never like to talk optimistic. A fellow who does in this business is just setting himself up for disappointment. Something always goes bad when you least expect it." He brooded through the night.

The next day, he went out and ran furiously just as if there was a chance. For forty laps. Then he threw a wheel, brought his three-cornered car to a stop and kicked at the wheel angrily as it rolled past him. He walked back to the pits where Dean and Brawner, frustrated again after fourteen years, waited. Softly, bitterly, Andretti said, "You work, work, work and then something happens like yesterday.

You dream about tomorrow and then tomorrow turns out to be like any other day." Brawner said, "Tomorrow. Next year. You keep trying." Al Dean did not say anything. He sat quietly, staring off into space. He did not know his last chance had gone. In a few months, he would die.

Jim Clark broke down early. And Clark would be killed in a crash in Germany before the next 500. Graham Hill broke down early. Gurney and Foyt were the only ones pursuing Jones with any passion and they kept falling further and further back. At 130 miles, Jones tried to get by Lee Roy Yarbrough to lap him and made contact and went into a side-by-side spin with him as the crowd screamed. Somehow, Jones avoided further contact, straightened out and resumed running and pulling away again.

At 400 miles, Gurney's car broke down. Then only Foyt was on the same lap with Jones, and he was fifty seconds behind. At 480 miles, Foyt was a full minute back. Then Gordon Johncock spun out and the yellow lights blinked on and the cars went into a slowdown period under caution. Round and round they ran, single file, in place, as the race ran out. In their pits, the Granatelli crew were jumping around in excitement, ready to celebrate their long-awaited victory, but flashing Parnelli an E-Z sign chalked on a blackboard to make sure he did not run any risks he did not have to run.

With three laps to go, the track was cleared and the green lights came on again and Parnelli picked up the pace a bit. Eight miles from home, as Jones was coming out of a turn, a ball bearing gave way in his gearbox, setting off a startling racket and leaving him without any power. Confused and shaken, he sat in his car and steered it as it coasted through the corner and down the backstretch. As the crowd saw him slowing down, the fans roared and Foyt heard it and saw some fans waving him on. Hope surged in him. Granatelli also heard the crowd and peered anxiously down the track. Hope faded in him.

As Parnelli glided down the mainstretch and into the pits, where he parked, Foyt sped past him, surprised and thrilled, into the lead. Granatelli sat on the pit wall beside his brothers Vince and Joe, his head down. "The years. All the years," he said. Then he said no more, sitting silently, gazing at the hot pavement. Parnelli sat on the ground and began to smoke a cigarette. After awhile, they got up and began to walk to their garage.

They did not even turn around as the crowd roared. Foyt came around on his last lap, and five cars tangled in front of him. Suddenly, wreckage was flying around the track and smoke and dust were rising. Somehow, Foyt got through it. He braked and slowed and picked his way through and came out of the corner and down the homestretch to his third 500 triumph, as many as any man ever has won.

In Granatelli's garage, Andy said, "They'll try to ban it now," he said. "They'll try to change the rules so we can't run it."

At the Victory Dinner, a new record of $734,846 was distributed. Foyt's car received $171,227. Andretti placed thirtieth and received $21,098.

Despite the tremendous advantage Foyt had gained in the championship circuit standings, a frustrated Andretti set out determinedly to overhaul him. Perhaps he pushed too hard. In practice at Milwaukee, he was running right behind Carl Williams when Carl's car threw a wheel. Trying to avoid him, Andretti rammed a wall, ending his hopes for that day. But Johncock, not Foyt, won the race.

Driving for Ford, Foyt and Gurney teamed to win the Twenty-Four Hours of LeMans in France. Andretti drove there, too, but crashed and was banged up. Testing at Mossport, Canada, he crashed and was shaken up further. Returning to the title trail at Langhorne, an aching Andretti settled for third place, but it was Ruby and Al Unser who ran ahead of him, not Foyt. Foyt's cars were breaking down on the champion circuit.

Points are awarded in the Pikes Peak Hill Climb and Mario will try anything, so he tried and finished fourteenth when his front suspension broke. Wes Vandervoort won. In a two-part road race at Mossport, Canada, Andretti's car snapped a half-shaft at the start of the first race and Bobby Unser won. Starting twenty-first in the second heat, Andretti made up ten positions in the first two laps before he came apart. Again, Unser won.

Still, Andretti refused to surrender. Foyt had not been picking up many points and remained within reach. In the 150-mile Hoosier Grand Prix road race, Andretti drove wildly to win in a new record 113.6 miles per hour, more than ten miles per hour faster than the previous standard.

In the Langhorne 150, Mario ran to a new track record of 113.1 miles per hour and lapped everyone except runnerup Gordon Johncock. Afterwards he said, "I could have lapped him, too. But why? I don't want to be spectacular. I just want to win."

At Mt. Tremblant, Canada, in the Labatt 200 road race, a two-part race, Andretti led all seventy-two laps and won both one-hundred-mile heats over Foyt for his third straight triumph.

Andretti was hot in pursuit of a third consecutive national championship now and Foyt knew he was in trouble in his bid for an unprecedented fifth title. At Springfield, on the dirt, Foyt snapped Andretti's string as he outran him in a torrid test. In the Milwaukee 200 on a paved circuit, Mario bounced back with a victory, leading all the way. In the DuQuoin 100, back on the dirt, Foyt outran McCluskey and Andretti. It was tight now. Foyt led Andretti, 2,280 points to 2,180.

The troops convened at the Indiana State Fairgrounds for the Hoosier Hundred, the dirt classic which pays more than any race outside of the 500. This year, $67,000 was at stake. And so, perhaps, was the U. S. title, worth $12,500 in cash, but considerably more in prestige. On a harness-racing track that recently had been host to Lawrence Welk, steer-judging, cow-milking and freckle-counting contests during State Fair week, Foyt, Andretti, and the field resumed in the race which Andretti had won a year back when Foyt's car failed him at the finish. The old grandstands were jammed.

Foyt was confident, but Andretti was ready. He took the lead early and held it for the last eighty-six laps during which he never was threatened, not even by Foyt, and won by a quarter-mile over A. J. He drove the dirt like it was home to him, averaged 95.5 m.p.h. and picked up $28,104 and 200 points, forty more than Foyt, and a crystal bowl, a sterling silver cup, a diamond ring, a blue jacket, and a kiss from a beauty queen.

Mario later classed it as one of his greatest thrills. He was lucky the year before, but not this year. "I beat him out in a pure, real race. Even A. J. admitted that I really won this one.

Foyt is one of the best there is on dirt. Beating him in the Hoosier is a key point in my career." Still, Mario was not cocky about catching Foyt in the title chase. "It will go down to the last day, I think," he predicted. That was the Riverside 300, and Andretti was right.

In the Trenton 200, pole-winner Andretti and Lloyd Ruby tangled, spun, hit the outer wall and were wrecked. Foyt, who had had trouble in qualifying, charged from last starting position to first at the finish in a valuable triumph. On the dirt in the Sacramento 100, Foyt outran Andretti to the wire by six seconds. In the Hanford, California, 200, Andretti and Al Unser tangled, crashed, and were knocked out. Foyt broke down. Art Pollard and Joe Leonard, driving turbocars, led but ran out of fuel near the finish as Johncock won. In the Phoenix 300, it was Foyt who crashed, and Andretti led from start to finish and won, moving to within 320 points of Foyt with only the finale remaining.

In the Rex Mays 300 on the Riverside road course outside of Los Angeles, Andretti was in a position to win the title with a victory, worth 600 points, if Foyt finished far back. Both drivers seemed tense and determined going in. "I have a chance" Andretti said. Foyt shrugged, "He'll have to take it from me. I won't give it to him. I'm ahead and I'll do whatever I can to stay there."

There were some things he could do and he did them in one of the wildest races in the history of the old tour.

Driving the nine-turn, 2.6-mile road course masterfully, Andretti was duelling Gurney, Bobby Unser, and McCluskey for the lead early, far in front of Foyt, when Al Miller spun into A. J. and wrecked him. The rules permitted a driver to pick up points while driving relief, so Foyt, who had planned for such an emergency, leaped from his wreck and raced back to the pits to call in his team's sister car, driven by Jim Hurtubise. When he got there, he found the car broken down and being pushed away. Foyt still had an ace up his sleeve. He charged into McCluskey's pit and told them to call in their driver, who had agreed to turn over his car in such an emergency. McCluskey was leading Andretti and Gurney at the time, but he respected his bargain and went in and jumped out as Foyt jumped in and went out.

The switch dropped Foyt's new car back in the standings, but he immediately began to move it back up. Meanwhile, Gurney suffered a flat tire and had to pit and Andretti charged toward victory. With a victory, he would become champion again. With a victory, he would pick up enough points to finish ahead of what Foyt would reach in relief. With only three miles to go and the valuable victory in his grasp and the noise of the crowd banging down on his helmet, Andretti's car ran out of fuel. A miscalculation! Cursing, he coasted into the pits. Bobby Unser surged by. Then Gurney surged by Unser. Hurriedly refueled, Andretti raced back out, but there was only one lap left. Gurney finished first. Unser second. Andretti third. Ruby fourth. Foyt, in McCluskey's car, fifth.

"I feel like crying. Only I'm too big to cry," the tiny Andretti sighed as he wiped the dirt from his drawn face and watched Gurney whoop it up in the victory circle. It would be awhile before USAC officials figured up the precise number of points, but Andretti knew it would be enough to have held him off. It was. Foyt was awarded 160 points and McCluskey 140 for their 300-point ride. Andretti gained 420 points with his third-place drive. Foyt finished with 3,440 points, eighty points ahead of Andretti's 3,360.

Now it was Foyt who was accused of having won cheaply. He had taken advantage of questionable rules. He could have cared less. "Those are the rules," he said, grinning. Andretti agreed. "I don't like the rules, but we live by them. In Foyt's position, I'd have done the same thing," he admitted. "I am disappointed. It has not been my year."

He had won eight championship events, and $108,306, in USAC races alone. Foyt had won five races, but two were big ones, and earned a record $233,563 and a fifth U. S. crown. He had won the Indianapolis 500 and the Twenty-four Hours of LeMans and the national title in the same year, a rare year for any racer. Andretti said, "There's always next year."

There was no next year for Al Dean. He died at sixty-one, of lung cancer. His teams had won more championship races, thirty-seven, and more national titles, five, than any other ever, but never Indy. Fifteen years of frustration had ended for him.

7. And Still Frustrated

IN 1965, after Mario Andretti won his first national championship, he was booked for an appearance on Joey Bishop's nationally televised late-night show. He was introduced not as the national driving champion, but as "The rookie of the year in the Indianapolis 500." This stuck in his mind. In the following years as he won another national title and narrowly missed a third, but broke down badly at Indy, he was aware how his failures there reduced his stature as a racer.

"It is not right that this one race should be worth more than all the other races combined," he mourned, "but it is, and you have to face that fact. Winning the national championship should be the biggest thing, and winning it two years in a row, as I did, should be bigger yet, but it isn't. Until I win Indy, it's like I win nothing."

He would not admit Indianapolis was so tough a challenge. He said other races and other tracks were tougher, but circumstances made Indy formidable. "A long dirt race is just as tough," he said. 'Driving one hundred miles at Langhorne, which is built so it's really just one long turn without any straights to relax on, is just as tough. A sports car race where you alternate driving for twelve or twenty-four hours through day and night and maybe through rain, and there is no letup, is just as tough. A Grand Prix race on a hard course through rain is just as tough. But Indy psychs everyone. The money you make there is so much more than any of the others. And the prestige you can gain. Winning the Indianapolis 500 just once seems to set a man apart and sets him up for life."

He shook his head and sighed, "Whatever you think, whatever you do for eleven months of the year, you always have Indianapolis in the back of your mind. In a way, you spend all your time planning and practicing for the 500. You keep racing, but your eye is always on the next 500. In May it eats you up. The greatest drivers and mechanics and the best and most expensive machinery are there and the competition is incredible. At no other race is a month spent getting ready. Then, in one day, in a few hours, it's suddenly all over, and one guy has won and the rest of them want to take the gas-pipe. The thing is such that until I win this one I will not really be satisfied with what I have done as a driver."

Having finished third, eighteenth, and thirtieth in his three years at Indianapolis, Andretti seemed to be going backwards steadily. As he entered the 1968 season, he was concentrating heavily on the classic. Al Dean was dead. Sadly, it never could be his. It still could be Mario's, and Clint Brawner's, too. Brawner had turned the wrenches on more championship trail winners than any other mechanic, but the big one had escaped him. It meant as much to him as anyone.

Andretti had stuck by Dean and Brawner. Now that Dean was gone, Andretti and Brawner decided to buy the equipment from the Dean estate and race it themselves, seeking a sponsor to back them. Years ago, it was possible for a driver and mechanic to operate independently, and if they were good enough and won enough, to do well. Along with the rise in the costs of living, there had been a rise in the cost of racing which in the 1960's made independence virtually impossible. It had reached the point where without the support of the major automotive firms, a racing team had trouble surviving, much less prospering. Andretti and Brawner had some support from Firestone and Ford and other companies, and they secured a strong sponsor, Overseas National Airways, but it still was a struggle for them.

Usually it takes a new car to win the 500. A chassis for a new car costs about $35,000. A new racing engine costs about $20,000. Usually there is a backup car worth about $20,000, in case of an accident. This has to have an engine. And, usually, a team will carry a spare engine in case the first one blows up. Tires alone for the month of May may run $2,000. A station wagon and trailer to haul the equipment around runs about $10,000 each. Some top drivers are guaranteed $100,000. You can't hire a good one for much less than $35,000. And he'll get forty to fifty per cent of the winnings. A top mechanic gets $15,000 or more and he'll get fifteen per cent of the winnings. Extra crewmen must be paid. Living expenses must be met. It all comes to around a quarter of a million dollars.

Most top teams put two cars on the track. Thus, Andy Granatelli estimates it costs $500,000 to mount a real Indy bid. There is only around $750,000 at stake at Indy, around

$1,000,000 throughout the title circuit. Even if a team ran one–two at Indy, it would only collect about $250,000, and if it kept winning throughout the circuit, could only hope to make about $350,000. Even if a team operated economically, built its own cars and cut costs wherever possible, it could not put a car on the track for much less than $150,000, so its chances of breaking even were rather slim.

The payoff must come in thrills, satisfaction, and advertising and promotional rewards. There are men hooked on the narcotic of racing willing to write off heavy expenses, but the number of these true sportsmen is dwindling rapidly as costs mount. Without the automotive firms' support, racing would dwindle. The manufacturers of cars, engines, tires, fuel, shock absorbers, spark plugs, and so forth bankroll racing. One may spend $100,000 to have a top car carrying its name. Another may spend $25,000 and all of its product the car can use simply to have it used, advertised, and, in the case of victories, promoted. Andretti's Overseas National Airways Special in 1968 carried around thirty decals of sponsors on its sides.

Indianapolis Motor Speedway never reveals its paid attendance or receipts, but it is estimated that its gross receipts run to about $6,000,000 for its one race annually. Ticket prices range from five dollars for standing room in the infield to thirty-five dollars for penthouse pews. There are more than 200,000 permanent seats and these are all sold out months before the race. It is estimated that more than 300,000 persons crowd their way into the grounds for the race. Another 200,000 at two dollars a head attend the opening day of qualifications. Another 150,000 attend the remaining three days. With crowds on practice days, close to 1,000,000 persons pay their way into the grounds during May. However, no one complains that Speedway president Tony Hulman is making unreasonable profits. Taxes are heavy. Money is plowed back into the track for improvements and new stands every year. And under Hulman's administration, payoffs are approaching $1,000,000 each race.

Andretti's drive to become king of this place as well as of racing in general began on the championship trail in 1968 at Hanford. Driving a new Ford-powered Brawner-Hawk, he contended for the lead until the rear-end collapsed on the fortieth lap and Johncock went on to win. In the Stardust 150, staged on the Las Vegas road track, he was on his way to winning when he had to pit for fuel with only five laps to go and Bobby Unser passed him for the triumph. "There is no reason in the world why that hog shouldn't have made it all the way on one tank," Mario mourned. However, in the wake of the turbine development, most teams were experimenting with turbocharged Ford and Offenshauser engines and these had not been perfected and were gulping huge amounts of fuel.

At Phoenix, Andretti crashed and was sidelined as Bobby Unser won again. At Trenton, Unser outran Andretti by three seconds. Suddenly Bobby Unser, heir to a great racing heritage, whose family had dominated the Pikes Peak Hill Climb for years, and whose brother, Al, had finished second in the previous Indianapolis 500, was the hot driver on the circuit, not Andretti and not Foyt. Still, this was not considered the year when a Bobby Unser with a turbocharged Offy perking perfectly went charging into the 500 regarded as the new favorite, but rather as the second year of Andy Granatelli's turbocar project, which still monopolized all attention.

As Granatelli had predicted, USAC had indeed put through new rules modifying turbine engines, and Granatelli had sued, and lost in court. But now he had returned to Indy with new, modified turbocars put together by England's Colin Chapman, and these seemed even faster than the first models.

Parnelli Jones had decided not to drive the turbocar again, nor to run the 500, but Granatelli had lined up a formidable team, including Grand Prix champions Jim Clark and Graham Hill. When Clark was killed in Germany, Mike Spence of Britain, a promising Grand Prix driver, replaced him. Then Spence lost control of one of the tricky turbocars in practice at Indianapolis, crashed it, and was killed. Chapman at first announced he would discontinue his participation in the project, then returned to it. Parnelli was cosponsoring cars with his old boss, J. C. Agajanian, and he permitted one of his drivers, Joe Leonard, a former motorcycle champion, to join the turbocar team.

Despite its fatal troubles, as qualifying began the new turbocars still had the rest of the fraternity nervous. Andretti had drawn a late run and while waiting for it, he paced his garage like a caged lion, while ten mechanics labored over his machine. He leaned against a wall, his hands behind his back, studying the floor. He pushed away and walked back and forth. Outside, the crowd began to roar. Someone came in to say that Graham Hill in one of the Granatelli turbocars had surpassed Mario's old records with one lap at 171.8 and a four-lap average at 171.2. Mario leaned against the wall again. He waited. A tremendous roar went up from the outside. Mario pushed through the crowd at the door of his garage and leaned out, trying to hear what was being said over the public address system.

"It was Leonard," someone said. "The other turbocar. A high 171."

Mario frowned and moved back inside.

"What was it?" a mechanic asked him.

"Leonard," he said softly. "A high 171."

"Can you beat it?" he was asked.

"Yeah, I can beat it," Mario said. But then he made a face as if he did not believe it.

He could not. Every year at Indianapolis you must go faster. Leonard had set the new records at 171.953 for one lap and 171.559 for four. Andretti went out and ran four of the most nearly identical laps anyone ever ran, 53.63, 53.57, 53.70 and 53.78 seconds, speeds of 167.817, 168.004, 167.598 and 167.348 for an average of 167.691, but for the first time in his four years at the Speedway he had not run faster than every man ahead of him and he did not get the record for even a little while. Nor did he have the pole, or even the first row, as Bobby Unser came in at 169.5 to bump Andretti down to fourth fastest, inside second row starting position.

Still, he was in and high, and after a morning replacing fouled spark-plugs, he was not totally dissatisfied. "We're close to the front. We can win from where we are if the turbocar will let us," he said. "Our Turbo-Ford has a lot of potential. It has a tremendous amount of power—more at the moment than we can use. If we can find the way to put some of what is left over now on the ground, we might surprise some people. We have a terrific automobile. No doubt about it. With the Turbo-Ford, it's a good combination. We just have to get everything working right.

"Aside from the turbocars, Bobby Unser's

the man to beat. And Foyt, of course. And Gurney. And Ruby, too." Ruby qualified fifth fastest, Foyt eighth, Gurney tenth. They were all in the show.

No one said it but you sensed that few were as afraid of Leonard and Hill in turbocars as they had been of Parnelli in a turbocar. So they waited and worried and dreamed through the remaining days to the race, including the remaining qualifying days.

The second Sunday and fourth qualifying day was rained out, and the field had not been filled, so an extra qualifying day was scheduled the Monday before Memorial Day to set eight more cars at the rear of the pack. On this day, Larry Dickson, driving for the Brawner-Andretti Overseas National Airways team, driving the old car Mario had driven to a record and put on the pole the year before, became the thirty-third and slowest qualifier. One car, from inside front row one year to outside rear row the next year, but with a different driver.

On this day, also, Bob Hurt crashed and was paralyzed, probably for life.

It rained virtually until race day, but race day was clear and warm. The track was dry. The bands marched. The music rang out. The bombs burst and the balloons flew. "Gentlemen, start your engines." The cars fired up and moved away.

The green flag flew. The turbocars took the

field into the first turn and the race was on. And in that very first lap, Andretti's engine began to misfire. He seemed to sag in his cockpit, unable to believe such misfortune could have stricken him again, and so swiftly. He coaxed the car through one lap, two laps, as the field pulled further and further away from him, but the pistons had come apart and the engine had gone sour and was giving him no power, and he coasted into the pits, cursing in his agony. He parked it and got out, looking like he could have killed it.

Desperately, he conferred with Brawner and they decided to call in their other car, the old car, and let Mario take it over from Dickson. This was done. But by the time he was called in, Dickson had fallen far behind the leaders. And by the time the change was made, there was no hope of winning. There was no hope, anyway. The pistons in Dickson's car had begun to come apart. Andretti charged out in a hopeless pursuit of the field that ended in thirty laps as he coasted into the pits, gushing black smoke out of the tail-end of his crippled car. He got out. Brawner and he did not speak to each other. There was nothing to say. Indy had beaten them again.

On the track, Unser and Ruby surprisingly outran Leonard in a tight, tense contest most of the way. Hill, Gurney, and Foyt ran next, but far back. At 220 miles, Foyt's car gave out. At

325 miles, Hill's right front suspension collapsed and he put his turbocar into the wall. At 300 miles, Unser began to experience clutch problems and had trouble keeping up with Ruby and Leonard.

With sixty-five miles left and a twelve-second lead on Leonard, Ruby seemed headed for victory when a coil popped in his engine and he coasted to a stop, deeply disappointed. Then, Leonard led by eight seconds and the Granatelli crew began to dance around in its pits. For the second straight year, a turbocar seemed safely in front near the finish. Surely, nothing could happen to prevent its victory again.

With forty-five miles to go, Carl Williams hit a wall, his car caught fire and the yellow caution signals came on. Leonard led the slowdown parade through the last miles. As lap after lap passed, Unser was trapped in the procession and unable to gain ground. There were only twenty miles left when the track was cleared and the green signals sent the cars on their own again.

Leonard slammed on the accelerator. His turbocar lurched ahead. Then its engine died. As the vast crowd rose in hysteria, the red turbocar coasted into the infield and the stunned Unser sped past and into the lead. "I said, 'C'mon, Bobby, let's go while the sun is shining,'" a jubilant Unser recalled later.

As Andretti has said, racing is the most unpredictable of sports. Stunningly, the turbocars had been struck down in the stretch a second straight year. In his pits, Andy Granatelli's shoulders slumped in disbelief and despair as the crowd laughed at the fat man's discomfort. He sank to the ground, his legs hiked up, his head hung between his knees. Later, it would be found that the fuel pump had failed. If you can't finish, you can't win. The turbocars may have been marvels, but they fell short of the finish.

Unser won it, and at the Victory Banquet he picked up $177,523 for his team. Gurney, finishing second, picked up $64,678. And he had the consolation of having built both his and Unser's car, Eagles. For Andretti, there was no consolation. He had hit the bottom now, the first car to retire, placed thirty-third and last, collecting $9,843. In the other car, Dickson's, he placed twenty-ninth. The two-time champion felt disgraced. "You dream a thousand dreams," he sighed.

All he and Brawner could do was go back to work and try somehow to catch Unser and regain the national title, try to win as much as possible, try to plan for the 1969 Indy so it would end differently from the others. "You just got to keep going," Andretti said. "You can quit or keep going. I was not about to quit."

At Milwaukee, Ronnie Duman crashed and was killed. Andretti led for awhile and finished second by two seconds behind Ruby. It was a roasting afternoon of racing, the temperature on the track ninety-three degrees and in the cockpits of these hot cars 125 degrees. "Heat is the hardest outside factor you have to deal with in racing," Andretti said, "It used to be worse with the front engine cars, with the heat coming up at you from the engine, but it's still bad in those cockpits. One year at Indy my hands developed blisters as big as pigeon eggs. The heat makes you weary and groggy and dulls your reflexes."

Still, they pressed on through the searing summer, the raw-boned Brawner wearing a bandana around his head and neck and a straw hat on his balding head to protect his sensitive skin from the sun. At Langhorne, Andretti's engine went sour a third of the way through and Johncock went on to beat out Bobby Unser. In a two-part road-race at Mosport Park, Canada, Andretti finished second to Gurney in both heats. Mario skidded almost out of control in the second heat, but somehow skillfully straightened out and salvaged points. At Pikes Peak, Andretti finished fourth, Bobby Unser first. At Castle Rock, Colorado, in the Rocky Mountain Road 150, Andretti broke down early and Foyt won. A highlight here was the fifth-place finish of Art Pollard in a turbocar, the first time one had finished a race.

In a rare night race on the new speedway in Mario's hometown of Nazareth, Al Unser won and Andretti had all he could do to outhustle young Bill Vukovich for second. At Indianapolis Raceway Park, Al outran Andretti in both halves of a two-part Hoosier Grand Prix. In twin 100's at Langhorne, Mario broke records in qualifying, but broke down before the qualifying ended, and Al Unser went on to sweep both parts, giving him five victories in a row. However, this was Al, not Bobby, who was breaking down often and failing to gain points.

In the two-part St. Jovite, Canada, road race, Andretti finally broke through for his first victories of the year, nosing out Al Unser by one second in the first heat and beating John Cannon by one minute in the second. After eight runnerup finishes, Mario was back in Victory Circle. However, at Springfield, his car broke down early as McCluskey scored. And in the Milwaukee 200, he blew victory when he had to refuel eighteen miles from home and was beaten out by Ruby.

At DuQuoin, on the dirt, he bounced back to outwrestle Foyt on his favorite turf. But in the Hoosier Hundred dirt classic, Foyt nosed him out. At Trenton Mario tried out a Turbo-Offy and returned to the winner's circle. It was a momentous day for Mario. His father, Alvise, fifty-nine years old, saw his first auto-race and saw his son win. "You better believe I'm proud," said Mario, remembering the years of turmoil. His father was proud, too.

At Sacramento, A. J. Foyt won, with Mario fourth. At Brookline, Michigan, in a 250-miler on the new two-mile Michigan International Speedway, Andretti was on his way to winning when he ran out of fuel near the finish and had to pit. Passed by Ron Bucknum, he finished second. It was disappointing, but it gave him enough points to pass Bobby Unser in the season's point standings. Actually, Unser, driving relief for Mike Mosely, seemed to have taken second at the finish, but Brawner posted a one-hundred-dollar bond to protest and after an official recheck of the scoring records, he was upheld and Andretti was moved up and into the lead in the title chase.

At Hanford, Foyt picked up his forty-first career victory, with Bobby Unser second and Andretti third. At Phoenix, Foyt and Andretti were swapping the lead back and forth when Foyt skidded on an oil slick, slammed into the homestretch wall, ricocheted 250 feet down the track sideways, and was rammed in the fuel tank by Andretti's car and burst into flames. Mario was able to get out of his car unaided, but Foyt, suffering burns, had to be helped from his car. Mario relieved George Snider and picked up points finishing third behind Gary Bettenhausen and Lloyd Ruby.

Again, the national championship hung on the finale at Riverside. This time, Andretti went in with a substantial lead of 315 points. This was a 300-miler with 600 points for the winner and 480 for the runnerup. If Mario finished first or second, it was all over again—he'd have another title. If Unser finished first or second, Mario still had only to finish in the first five to win. If he drove his own car, of course. If he drove relief, that was something else. He would be awarded points based on how much of the race he drove and where the car finished.

Having been burned by Foyt's relief rides of the year before, Andretti made extensive plans to go that way himself if necessary, this time. He and Brawner entered a second car, to be driven by Jerry Titus, and to be turned over to Mario if needed. And he arranged with Parnelli Jones to take over Joe Leonard's turbocar if that was needed. It was, and more. Mario drove hard and had just taken the lead from Gurney on the fifty-seventh lap when his engine blew apart and he had to coast into the pits. There he found his sister car already parked with engine failure.

Andretti rushed toward Jones's pit. Joe Leonard had just signalled Jones that his brakes were gone. As Andretti reached the pits, Leonard pulled in. As Leonard got out of the car, Andretti got in and pulled away. He did not know he did not have any brakes. He turned into the corner and promptly rammed Art Pollard's car, wrecking both turbocars in one fell swoop. Desperately, he grabbed a ride on Parnelli's motorcycle and rushed back to the pits and sought another relief ride. Lloyd Ruby's crew agreed, calling in Ruby. Andretti jumped in the car and took off.

By then, Gurney was far ahead and driving steadily. Unser was stroking smoothly in second place, a lap back. And that's the way they finished. Andretti drove the last forty-six laps in Ruby's car and, driving furiously, finished third.

The drama reverted to the men with the pencils, the officials who had to total up the points. Unser got his 480 points, of course. Andretti was awarded 165 of the 420 third-place points. Adding it all up, Unser had 4,330 points, Andretti 4,319. In the closest finish in the history of the championship circuit, Andretti had lost by eleven points.

"It worked for Foyt, but not for me," Mario sighed. "It's a bad rule. Even though I was ready to try anything, it's still a bad rule."

Bobby Unser had finished first five times and second five times on the tour and earned a record $261,124. Andretti had finished first four times and second eleven times and earned $109,102. Andretti now had won twenty-one championship races, but he still had not won the 500. He had won two straight national titles, then been nosed out narrowly for the next two.

"I would," he said, "trade three national championships for just one Indy victory."

8. The Versatile One

"THE thing I admire in a racing driver is versatility," Mario Andretti has said. "The ability to take any kind of car on any kind of track in any kind of race and do well with it against anyone. You may not always win, but if you get more out of the car or the track or the race than you should, well, the race drivers know. They know the real pros."

While dominating the championship circuit without dominating the Indianapolis 500, Mario Andretti demonstrated his versatility through the last half of the 1960's. Once, he beat his way up through the bushes he gradually began to drive the midget cars and sprint cars infrequently, primarily because they represented a big risk for little profit. However, he drove them well enough to finish third in USAC sprint car standings in 1964 and second in 1963.

He drove stock cars even less often, yet on one of his infrequent starts in one of these 4,000-pound, beefed-up, souped-up monster versions of the passenger cars we all drive, the little Andretti challenged the greatest of the southern stock-car drivers on the greatest of their super-speedways and won their Indianapolis, the Daytona 500.

This was in 1967, in February, when the rest of the country was still in winter and even Florida was chilly. When Ronney Householder of Chrysler was asked to assess Andretti's chances before the race, he said, bluntly, "Mario Andretti? No chance." He explained, "It takes a big, strong man to handle these stock cars on this track. He's just too small for this kind of traffic. The strain is too heavy."

On the first day of qualifying, old Curtis Turner rocketed a Chevrolet Chevelle around the two-and-one-half-mile high-banked course, which is faster than Indy because of the high banks, at 180.8, a record, which captured the pole starting position. On later days, five other drivers ran faster and the fastest of all was Andretti, who rocketed his Ford Fairlane around at 182.8.

Marvelling at the speeds, Andretti smilingly suggested, "No one can drive that fast without cheating."

Someone said, "But you're driving fastest of all."

Mario grinned and said, "Maybe I'm cheating."

On race day, a crowd of 94,250 persons, the largest in Florida sports history, jammed the grounds, and closed-circuit cameras focused on the race for the benefit of another 400,000 theater-television patrons around the country. Grand Ole Opry star Roy Drusky sang "Swanee River" and the race began, a demolition derby as much as a race.

Fifty cars, big cars, brightly painted and potent, started, sizzling around the steep saucer in tight traffic at incredible speed. First Turner led. Then Lee Roy Yarbrough. Then A. J. Foyt, another visitor from the north. Then Yarbrough again. Then Buddy Baker. The lead kept going back and forth. Before the day was done, nine different drivers would exchange the lead no less than thirty-seven times. It was incredibly competitive. Sometimes the leader was surpassed as he pitted. Sometimes, he simply was passed.

The first breakdown occurred on the first lap. The second on the second lap. The first crackup occurred on the fourth lap when Friday Hassler crashed. Twenty cars went out before the halfway point. Good drivers wrecked good cars. Paul Goldsmith slid back and forth across the track, sucking Cale Yarborough into a mishap. Dick Hutcherson's car ran over some metal, blew a tire and hit the wall. The race was slowed nine times under caution. Foyt's clutch went out. Richard Petty's suspension twisted. Lee Roy Yarbrough blew his engine. Buddy Baker blew his engine. Curtis Turner blew his engine. David Pearson blew his engine.

The pace was punishing, with the leaders turning laps in traffic above 180 miles per hour. At less than sixty miles per hour, a car simply would slide off the high banks. At 180, they threatened to take off like airplanes. Householder had suggested that, at 182 in qualifying, "Andretti couldn't hold his car on the track; he was all over the place." Later, Richard Petty said Andretti made him edgy because he was drifting so high in the corners. Other drivers have criticized Mario other times for moving up and down so much on race tracks.

Mario admitted it. "Every time I completed one lap, I wondered if I could complete another. Actually, I like to use all of a track, but I never jeopardize anyone's safety. In traffic I stayed in my lane, but when I was alone, I used all the track. I like to set a stocker up looser than some people and I guess it appeared to some I was on the edge of losing it going through the turns. I like to hang the rear end of my car out on the corners. I really went flat out all the way."

He took the lead for the first time on the twenty-third lap, lost it on the fortieth lap, regained it on the fifty-fifth, lost it on the seventy-seventh, regained it on the ninety-seventh, lost it on the ninety-eighth, regained it on the ninety-ninth. Around and around the big cars boomed—those that survived.

Andretti learned some lessons, especially about drafting, a tricky tailgating technique employed by big-car chauffeurs who poke the nose of their cars almost to the tails of the car ahead of them and are sucked along by them, saving fuel and adding speed. At great speed, this is touchy business. If the car in front of you stops, forget it. When you move out of the vacuum, it can be jolting. But if you accelerate as you do so, you can be sucked past him, virtually sling-shotted into the lead. Many NASCAR races are won by cars which enter the last lap in second place, drafting the leader, then slingshot past him off the last turn.

"I did less drafting than others," Mario said. At one point, seven cars were running nose to tail around the course and Mario was at the head of the pack. "It's very unnerving. When I was drafting, I felt as though I was sitting quietly, tied to a fencepost, not moving 180 miles per hour at all. But when I lost my leader, I felt an impact as though I had been slammed into a brick wall.

"I don't keep my line when someone is drafting me. I don't want anybody to know my line or what my problems are. I don't want him to know whether my front end or my back end is loose."

Secretive, the slick speedster kept pressing, out of the lead on the 115th lap, in it on the 127th, out on the 136th, back in it on the 143rd, out of it on the 144th, back in it on the 145th, out of it on the 153rd. It was a savage struggle. And there were times of tension. "I had a few anxious moments out there," Mario admitted later. "If I had to tell you about all of them, we would be here all night." In the last one hundred miles, he duelled with Darel Dieringer, David Pearson, and Freddie Lorenzen. When Dieringer dropped back and Pearson blew up, the lead came in the late stages to Lorenzen and Andretti. Lorenzen was a master of the high-banks, perhaps the greatest super-speedway stock-car driver in history. Everyone assumed he would overpower Andretti in the clutch.

Andretti regained the lead on the 159th lap.

Lorenzen took it on the 165th lap. Andretti took it back for the ninth time on the 168th lap. Pouring it on, he began to pull away. His lead went to a full second, two seconds, five seconds, seven seconds. Superbly prepared by the powerful southern mechanical team of Holman and Moody, Mario's car performed faultlessly. In the late stages, he was all by himself.

On the next-to-last lap, he had to get through a sticky situation. He was about to pass three cars in a bunch when one blew his engine and the others started slipping around in oil, and smoke obscured everyone's vision. Mario, blinded by the smoke, gambled on the high road, cutting to the wall and hanging there as he raced around the melee safely and sped through the final miles to win.

After three hours, twenty-four minutes and eleven seconds, he finished the two hundred laps at an average speed of 146.926 miles per hours and boomed happily into the winner's circle. He collected $43,000 of the $200,000 purse.

Later, he admitted, "This was the toughest race of my career. At these speeds, there isn't ever a chance to relax, even on the straightaway, because the varying air currents always make the car seem almost out of control. But I like to run at speed."

Asked if he would drive an Indianapolis car here, where it would run far over two hundred miles per hour—if it stayed on the track—Andretti shrugged, "If I did, it would cost someone an awful lot of money."

Studying, him, Kate Firestone of the tire family said, "Look at him! He's so teensy." And *Detroit News* writer Pete Waldmeir said, "He's toughsy and fastsy, too."

That same year, Andretti returned to Florida to race a Ford sports car in the Twelve Hours of Sebring endurance test, in which his car had touched off an accident fatal to four spectators the year before. He was teamed with Bruce McLaren, a standout on the sports-car circuit and an outstanding Grand Prix driver. Ferrari, for years the dominant team in sports-car racing, passed up the event and the potent American Chaparrals broke down early. Still, the task of Andretti and McLaren was formidable.

Carroll Shelby's crew had prepared the car perfectly. McLaren had the first stint and took the lead early, leading Foyt in another Ford he was sharing with Ruby, and Jim Hall and Mike Spence in a Chaparral, and Gerhard Mitter and Scooter Patrick in a Porsche. Andretti took over. Then McLaren. Then Andretti again. Darkness fell. The fans ate and drank and built bonfires and the cars roared round and round the twisting course.

Andretti and McLaren held the lead most of the way, driving methodically, but brilliantly.

"It's a hard race," Andretti commented. "Most of the way flat out. You go and go and go and even when you're out of the car you don't seem able to rest. It doesn't seem like it's ever going to end."

But, it did. After twelve hours, having covered 1,237 miles at an average speed of 102.9 miles per hour, a record, the Andretti-McLaren machine took the checkered flag and the two drivers took the congratulations and drank champagne.

After winning the Daytona 500, Andretti smiled and said, "I don't think NASCAR guys are too happy about a USAC guy taking their pet race." After winning the Sebring Enduro, he pointed out proudly, "There were some in the so-called sporty set that seemed to think that a USAC guy couldn't make it in a tough road race. I don't mean to say that all sports car people think this way, but there have always been some snobs in any kind of racing. It's like certain guys in USAC who are always putting down the road-racing guys who come to Indy."

Mario says, "Jim Clark was one of the greatest Indy drivers I ever saw. Jackie Stewart, Graham Hill, Denny Hulme and Dan Gurney proved themselves. These are great sports-car and Grand Prix drivers. Of course most drivers are at their best on their home grounds. A fellow like Richard Petty is a pretty tough guy to beat in a stock-car race. Roger McCluskey is a pretty tough guy to beat in a sprint-car race. Or any kind of race. A. J. Foyt is pretty tough to beat on dirt. Or on any surface. In anything. Parnelli Jones was tough to beat on anything and in anything, and still is when he races.

"The great ones," says Mario, "drive anything."

After Sebring, Mario took a try at the ultimate in the endurance classics, the Twenty-four Hours of LeMans in France. It was a race won by Foyt and Gurney.

At three in the morning, the brakes on Mario's Ford grabbed as he entered a turn at 150 miles per hour. He spun, crashed off of outside and inside barriers, and ground to a halt in the middle of the track. Badly battered, he scrambled out to safety atop a wall. Meanwhile sister cars driven by McCluskey and Jo Schlesser, coming round the bend and onto his stalled machine, ploughed into barriers to avoid hitting him.

"I'll do it again and I hope just once," Mario said.

"I'd like to win it because it's a classic. I'd like to have one good memory from LeMans. Then I'd quit it for sure. I'd like to say I love LeMans, but I don't. It's a tremendously dangerous race. There are no safety features to speak of, and that should be unheard of nowadays."

Three days later, hurting but unafraid, he

was back in the U. S. and almost won a championship race.

A much more burning ambition of Mario's is to win a Grand Prix race, especially the Grand Prix of Italy. For a European-born driver, an Italian-born driver, one who grew up worshipping Grand Prix drivers and dreaming of Grand Prix glory, this is understandable. The demands of his championship circuit have curtailed these ambitions, but Andretti has had offers, from Ferrari and others, and has seized the opportunity to try Grand Prix races on occasion.

Once, Andretti and Bobby Unser flew to Monza to qualify for the Italian Grand Prix only to be told he would not be permitted to race because he would be involved in another race the day before and their rules did not permit drivers to compete on consecutive days. Andretti, who had been the fastest driver in practice, was quite bitter about it, since he often drove on consecutive days in the U. S. "Heck, I could have slept on the plane," he smiled sarcastically.

Another time, Andretti entered the U. S. Grand Prix at Watkins Glen, New York. Driving a Lotus Ford, Mario startled the sporty set by whipping his sleek Formula One creation around the winding, hilly course at 130 m.p.h., faster than the finest, to bump Scot Jackie Stewart off the pole.

On race day, a record crowd of more than

90,000 persons crammed the countryside. Andretti led the first lap, but lost it on the second lap when he brushed a hay bale and knocked his car's nose apart. He held second for thirteen laps, when he finally made a pit stop to have the nose repaired. Resuming, he had fallen into thirteenth place. In one lap, he was twelfth. In another, eleventh. Soon he was tenth. Then ninth. Then his gearbox collapsed and he was out of the race.

"It was a big kick," he said. "My Lotus didn't last long, but it was a big boot while it did." Wistfully, he suggested some day he might be tempted to give it a more thorough trial, even if it represented a financial sacrifice. "It is a challenge and I'm not sure I'd rest easy if I didn't try harder to win at least one Grand Prix race. And I can't say I don't think I wouldn't enjoy the European tour.

"It's a matter of being practical. The money, for me, anyway, is here. I live here. I'm an American now, and proud of it. And I'd hate to be away from my family any length of time. But that glamorous circuit is a temptation."

More than fifty years ago, U. S. and Indianapolis champion Jimmy Murphy won the French Grand Prix. The next American to win a Grand Prix race was Phil Hill, who won the Grand Prix championship in 1961. Later Dan Gurney won a number of Grand Prix races and Richie Ginther won one. And Hill participated in three LeMans victories and Gurney in one, with Foyt. But Hill and Ginther never dared the championship circuit. Gurney did, and won championship races, though through the end of the 1960's, despite consecutive second-place finishes, never the Indianapolis 500.

Foyt won LeMans and Nassau in sports cars, two Firecracker 400's at Daytona, one Riverside 500 road race in stock cars, and the Indianapolis 500 three times, and more championship circuit races than any other driver ever, forty-two, and more national titles, five, through the first month of 1970. He never had tried a Grand Prix race. Andretti won Sebring and as the 1960's ran out he had won three national titles and was threatening to surpass Foyt in titles and title races won. As 1969 began he was hopeful of becoming the only driver ever to win both of America's supreme racing tests, the Daytona 500 stock-car classic, which he had won, and the Indianapolis 500 championship-car classic, which he had not.

9. King
of
Indy

"I'LL beat this place," Mario Andretti said one day in May of 1969 as he sat on the pit wall of the Indianapolis Motor Speedway, hiding his eyes behind sunglasses. "I'll do whatever I have to do. I'll beat this place if it takes all my life."

After Mario's impressive rookie performance in the 500 in 1965, Andy Granatelli sought to sign him as a driver for his exotic Novi racing cars. Politely, Mario declined. Impolitely, Andy said, "You'll never win the 500 until you join up with me." He has that sort of ego, although he did not win the 500, or any other race on the championship trail in twenty years of trying with many cars, including the glamorous but ill-fated Novis, and two years of trying with the turbines.

Again, USAC had legislated against the turbines, this time so reducing its permissible power that Granatelli grudgingly abandoned the project. Andy returned to more standard racing cars, including three Lotus-Fords built in England by Colin Chapman. And he returned to Andretti as a driver.

While Andretti and Brawner had, unlike Granatelli, won consistently, they had, like Granatelli, never won Indy. They had, in fact, sunk to last place in the last race. They opened the 1969 season in financial trouble. Neither was personally poor, but neither was in a position to blow his wealth in support of a racing program that could not return them a profit. They had nothing to promote except themselves. Nor were they able to find sufficient sponsorship support from the promoters who were then available.

After Mario led, but broke down at Phoenix in a new Brawner-McGee Hawk, Mario and Clint turned to Andy and accepted his sponsorship. The deal was that he would buy their cars and equipment and they would operate his cars as a team under his sponsorship. Mario was guaranteed a salary of $100,000 and all the support he needed. Brawner and McGee were guaranteed salaries, promised support, and promised they would be permitted to do things their own way.

If Granatelli was bound to take credit for any success, such was only fair. It was his money that paid the bills, and, by his own estimate, he had invested $8,000,000 in racing over the years. At Andretti's insistence, Andy did agree to discontinue team uniforms so covered with STP emblems they looked like polka-dot pajamas. Still, STP decals and the slogan, "The Racer's Edge," turned up everywhere.

At Hanford, with the new Lotus-Fords still not ready, Mario drove a Brawner-Hawk for Granatelli and won for him—Andy's first victory. "We've broken his jinx," Mario said later, happily. "Maybe," said Granatelli, as the team turned toward Indy, "just maybe two losers will make a winner."

At Indy, Granatelli glowed. It was as though he had rejoined the family. "All the years, everyone loved me," he sighed. "All the time I was losing with the Novis, everyone loved me. Everyone said they were rooting for me to win. Maybe that's because they didn't think I would win. Then I brought the turbine and everyone hated me. All my old friends turned their backs on me. I was an outcast. Maybe that's because they didn't think I could lose. I had something different they didn't have and they were afraid they'd have to spend money to keep up with me. But what is this place, if not for change and improvement and progress? Well, whatever it is, it wasn't for the turbine. So I've had to go their way. And I'm everyone's friend again. Fine. I feel good about that. But I'll beat them. If I can't beat them on my terms, I'll beat them on theirs. I won't give up until I do."

Brawner looked across the track and said, "A sponsor is a sponsor. Granatelli is generous. He's honest. He keeps his bargains. He spent a lot of money and deserves a victory here. I've spent eighteen years trying to win here. If I win here, I'll retire." McGee said, "I'm a young fellow. I can wait. But I don't want to wait." Andretti said, "I want to win for Granatelli. I want to win for Brawner. I want to win for me. I wanted to win for Dean. I'm sorry I couldn't. Now I'll try to win for Granatelli. But Brawner and McGee will be turning the wrenches. And it'll be me in the cockpit, all alone in our car out there on the track."

The new Lotus-Fords arrived, assigned to Andretti, Graham Hill, and Jochen Rindt. Andy was the overall supervisor with other members of the Granatelli family, Vince and Joe, preparing the Hill and Rindt cars. There was plenty of money for everything. Everything was done first class.

Andretti's new Lotus had four-wheel drive,

which was different from the two-wheel drive of his Hawk, but he swiftly accustomed himself to it and soon was outrunning everyone in practice, as usual, turning laps around 171 and 172 miles per hour. As the opening weekend of qualifying drew near, Andretti was the heavy favorite to win the pole position for the third time. A. J. Foyt in a cigar-shaped Coyote-Ford he had built himself, and defending champion Bobby Unser in a Lola-Offy, were the only serious threats. Dan Gurney was running a souped-up stock Ford engine and was not considered a threat to the top speedsters.

Andretti never got a chance to win the pole position on the opening day of qualifications. It rained that day and the next day too. Only a few cars even got on the track and no one qualified. A driver named Jigger Sirois turned 161.2, but his sponsor, Myron Caves, waved him off before the run was completed, and everyone spent most of the next week arguing whether he might have won the pole position at that slow speed or whether thirty-three cars would have qualified faster on other days, bumping him off. Qualifying time was reduced to a final weekend.

At five P.M. on the Wednesday before qualifying, Foyt turned a lap above 172. Andretti went out to top him and as he was going through the fourth turn, his car's rear end collapsed, breaking off the right rear wheel. He spun one and a half turns, skidded 320 feet into the wall, ground along the wall for sixty feet as the car came apart in sections, spun off, slid 260 feet and scraped to a stop aflame in the middle of the track.

"All of a sudden, I was spinning. I knew I was going to hit hard. I tried to unbuckle my harness and hold my hands over my face. The fire was right over the cockpit," Andretti recalled later. By the time the car came off the wall, the body had ripped off and he was sitting in the stripped chassis, and the car was still sliding, but slowly, as he scrambled from it. "I wasn't even stopped and I was out of it," he said.

People were yelling and running at him. Granatelli said, "I had to figure he'd had it. I was sick with fear." Andretti was burned, but he was all right. He was loaded into an ambulance and rushed to the track hospital where he was treated for second-degree burns on his upper lip, his nose, and his cheeks, then released. Foyt was one of the first to visit him there. They are fierce foes more than friends, but they know what this thing is for each other.

Asked if he had been frightened, Andretti said, "I'm only human." Then he sighed and said, "I was lucky. You always feel lucky when you walk out of an accident. Anytime you can race tomorrow, you have to feel lucky." Art Pollard who had been driving on the track immediately behind the accident, said, "It was the worst wreck I ever saw. You had to figure there were four or five cars involved, there was so much debris being thrown around. I couldn't imagine anyone surviving it."

The car was demolished, but Granatelli said, "I'm lucky. You can always buy a new machine, but you can't replace people. And in this whole world there is only one Mario Andretti." Dee Ann Andretti, who cried with shock and relief, agreed.

Granatelli, Chapman, Brawner, McGee, and Andretti and others on the team huddled. USAC officials decided they would examine the rear ends of the remaining Lotus Fords before permitting them to continue. But it didn't matter, for the team decided to retire them on a precautionary basis, sidelining Hill and Rindt. Andretti still had his Hawk. He now was not interested in one of the other Lotus-Fords.

"I'm as brave as the next guy, but only if I'm satisfied the car is safe. My crew doesn't want to bolt me into just any old tub. I don't, either." Privately he admitted, "I felt the race was all over. I'd been hexed again."

There was never any doubt Andretti would run anyway. All this time everyone had been saying no one would ever know how good a race-driver he really was until he came back from a bad accident, and now he'd had a real bad one and now he would show them. He says he didn't feel nervous. This was his life and he was used to it. He did have to re-condition himself to his Hawk, and it had to be swiftly set up for this special race, but he had won Hanford in it, and he did admit, when he sat in it again, "I felt like I had gotten home." It was a comfortable car, but not an overpowering one.

The day after the accident, his face burnt raw and sore and painful, he was back on the track again, swiftly working his Hawk up to 171, surprising and pleasing everyone. Brawner and the team had two days to get it ready and they worked hard at it, and Andretti practiced it to points of perfection. Still, there was little hope of regaining the pole position. There simply was not time to get it on tap, though Andretti approached it. On the morning of the time trials, as the crowd settled into the stands, Mario kept walking around the car and studying it and touching it as if to make a friend of it. The blood-red STP Oil Treatment Special Number Two waited.

Foyt was too fast, forcing his Coyote around the oval at an average speed of 170.568 miles per hour, with a fast lap of 171.625, which was the fastest any piston-engine car had ever gone at the old track, though not as fast as the two turbine cars had gone a year earlier. Andretti came amazingly close under the circumstances. As usual, he toured the track with stunning consistency, in 52.80, 53.28, 52.87, and 53.00

seconds, every lap within a half-second of every other lap, for speeds of 170.455, 168.918, 170.229, and 169.811, and an average of 169.851, good for second spot, front row center. Unser took the outside slot at 169.683.

Rookie Mark Donohue and veterans Gordon Johncock and Roger McCluskey filled the second row. McElreath wound up in the third row, Gurney and Leonard in the fourth row, and Lloyd Ruby further back. When the field was filled on Sunday, the thirty-third and slowest to make the starting field was Peter Revson, at 160.8, which was slower than Sirois had gone on the first rainy day. Sirois never made it, though if he had taken his time that day, he'd have started on the pole, a freaky thing, and would have been a celebrity forever. Among those on the sidelines were Parnelli Jones and Al Unser. Jones was sponsoring cars at Indy now, not driving them, but Unser, who was supposed to drive for him, had broken his leg fooling around on a motorcycle at the track, blowing a shot at a fortune. It is an accomplishment just to make this race. Many good drivers never do.

Andretti was starting up front, from where he could win, but he did not think he would win. In practice the car developed serious problems. When it was run many laps above 168, the turbocharged Ford engine overheated badly and consumed huge quantities of fuel. Even under ideal circumstances, these high-powered monsters boil and consume a gallon of fuel every two miles, but Andretti's car was roasting and gulping almost two gallons a lap. Fuel tank capacity is limited to seventy-five gallons and no one could make more than three pit stops and hope to win, so it seemed Mario had no hope.

Brawner and McGee devised a rich fuel blend which would go the limit if they took the time to fill the tanks to the top every stop and did not run too fast and too hot, though of course the idea at Indy is to run fast.

They asked for and received permission from chief steward Harlan Fengler to add an external radiator which they felt might cool the engine sufficiently for success. However, there was a rule forbidding external changes between qualifying and race day, which was not always enforced, and Foyt protested that since he had worked long and hard to rig up an extra internal radiator before qualifying, Andretti should not be permitted to break the rule later. After conferring with other officials, Fengler told Andretti he was sorry, but he'd have to revoke his permission and the radiator would have to be removed.

Andretti was very angry and threatened to withdraw the car. Reportedly, Fengler said to Mario, "This Speedway made you what you are today," and Mario retorted, "If I had to depend on this place for a living, I'd starve." Later, Mario said, "We'll run, but it's stupid. We won't last twenty laps." Again, as after the accident, he figured they were whipped.

Foyt was the favorite then and Andretti was very tense as the race approached. The night before the race he got into a minor fuss with Dee Ann over some unimportant matter and hollered at her and she cried. She was seven months pregnant and had their two sons with her and she was as tense as he was. On race day, she left the boys with a baby-sitter, figuring they were too young to be involved in Speedway strain, and went herself, sitting with a friend.

The partying around town had been going on for days and nights. Through the night before the race, the row of cars built up outside the Speedway waiting for it to open up. The fans danced to transistor radios and played cards and drank beer and soft drinks and slept in cars and trucks and on the grass.

Before dawn, the gates were thrown open and the great crowd began to move in. They came by plane and bus and car from all over the country and surrounding cities, an enormous crowd, larger than all but our largest cities, more than 300,000 persons, filling the sprawling arena and the huge stands. The cars sat silently in their garages as the mechanics and drivers waited.

The bands began to march around the track. Music filled the spring air. The day warmed up until it was hot, which bothered the drivers. Eventually, it would reach eighty-five degrees, which meant 125 degrees inside the cockpits of the cars. The cars were pushed to the pit apron, where they waited some more. The songs were sung: "Back Home Again In Indiana," "On The Banks Of The Wabash," "The Star Spangled Banner." A bugler played "Taps," in honor of the war dead, on this Memorial Day, and the racing dead. Across the country, nearly a million persons filled theaters to see the closed-circuit telecast.

The cars were pushed onto the track where they waited. The crews and drivers stood by them waiting. Waiting, waiting. The tension thickened. There is nothing quite like it in sports, this deadly dance of dreams, this cruel carnival of speed and wealth. The drivers considered their chances, plotting their paths to glory. They are, really, the greatest of athletes and bravest of men. They must have all that other athletes have—skill and stamina and quickness—but they, unlike most men, must perform their professions with daring at great risk in constant peril. Counselled by his crew, Andretti was prepared to restrain himself. Always a charger, he knew his only hope would be to drive conservatively. He had said, "Racing is charging." Now he said, "I have to drive a second-place race if I hope to finish first." He strapped himself in, a bandanna over his sore and blistered face, not thinking about the pain.

He really had little hope as the fake bombs burst and the balloons flew into the air and Tony Hulman took a microphone and, into a sudden hush, said the magic words, "Gentlemen, start your engines." The words and the sudden roaring up of the engines thrilled the fans, as always, and the gaudily painted, nimble, expensive cars moved away, settling into position on the warmup laps.

Before the race, Unser had stopped by Andretti's garage and warned Mario it might be unwise to try to take the lead from Foyt at the first turn. "Foyt wants it real bad, so don't do anything foolish," he said. And Andretti said, "I wasn't going to squeeze anybody. That could be tragic." Now, however, as the green flag flew and the cars accelerated into that incredible roaring tangle through the first turn, it was Andretti who flashed in front. "I just accelerated normally and was surprised no one ran faster," he said later.

He held the lead through the first five laps. "I wanted to see how strong I could run before the thing heated up too much. I felt maybe after twenty, twenty-five laps it would be all over for me," he explained later. "I drove by the gauges. In a few laps, the car began to overheat and I figured I was cooked. Water started to slosh into the cockpit and I had to ease off, and Foyt flew by me. But then I found that when the water gauge got to 220 degrees and the oil to 240, it sort of levelled off and I could hold it in balance there as long as I didn't run faster, which was around 165, and I just had to hope that was fast enough."

At first it was not. Foyt was flying out front and then McCluskey got past Mario, too. "It was quite a temptation to race them, but I kept telling myself I didn't dare to," Andretti recalls. Unser was having handling problems with his car and was wearing out his tires and was struggling, but Ruby was working his way up through the pack to threaten the leaders and on the fortieth lap he got past Andretti and McCluskey to take second. On the forty-eighth lap, McCluskey had run out of fuel unexpectedly, so he had to coast into the pits and by the time he got in and out he was far back and out of contention.

Andretti had to gamble on stretching his fuel to the ultimate, but as he passed the fiftieth lap, he was still running, which was a lot more than the previous year—when he lasted two laps—so he was encouraged. He went in for fuel and stayed in forty-three seconds, which is twice as long as normal. It cost him a lot of ground on the track, but he had to be sure he got a full tank, because he needed every drop. He resumed racing well behind Ruby and much further behind Foyt, who was flying, cheered on by the crowd, which rooted for him to make history by becoming the first man ever to win this fierce test a fourth time. Of course, Andretti had his supporters who wanted him to win it a first time.

It wasn't to be for Foyt. His engine cracked and on the seventy-ninth lap, he pitted. He didn't park it, but waited to have repairs made so he could resume running. He couldn't win then, but he still wanted to run, which he did, and finished eighth, eventually. With the tough Texan removed as a competitor, another Texan, forty-one-year-old Ruby, the hard-luck character of this classic, ran in front. Andretti passed him at one point, but was passed by him again on the 104th lap when he made his second pit stop—another long one, thirty-nine seconds—which left him far back again when he resumed.

It was a pleasantly safe race. McElreath's car caught fire and he parked it, and Arnie Knepper's car broke and he put it on a wall, but both got out in good shape and those were the only two caution periods. A lot of cars were breaking down, but the survivors rolled on smoothly as the day wore on and the fans were baked by the sun and the drivers were roasted in their cockpits and all were made sweaty and weary and dazed by the relentless, almost monotonous merry-go-round. On the 108th lap, however, came the break of the race.

Ruby pitted for his second stop. Fueling is done into twin tanks by two hoses. These lock onto the tanks to prevent risky spillage, then when fueling is completed, are swiftly unlocked and the driver is whacked on the helmet or back as a signal to speed out. As fueling of Ruby's car was completed, one of his crew hit him on the helmet and he accelerated. But one of the hoses had not been unlocked. The side of the tank was torn out and fuel gushed onto the ground and Ruby's blood seemed to drain with it. He banged on the brakes almost immediately, but it was too late. For the third year in a row, he had lost the race in the lead. His crew chief Dave Laycock stormed off and tore up a water cooler in anger. Ruby got out and walked away and said, "I guess it just isn't meant for me to win in this place."

It is a cruel place, to be sure, and it had been harder on no one than it had been on Andretti, but now, suddenly, he led, and as he rolled into his 112th lap, he had gone further than he had the three previous years put together. All the fast cars were out by then, and the closest cars to Andretti, those of Gurney and Unser, were well back and struggling. And there still was a long way to go, more than two hundred miles. If anyone pressed Mario, he would overheat and run dry. Dee Ann Andretti watched silently, gripping the green rail in front of her seat and chewing the wax off a soft-drink cup, while the crowd around her roared.

The Granatelli crew jerked around nervously. Andretti was running conservatively at 165 but he seemed all over the track, high and low, making passes as he lapped cars in traffic. It's his way, he says, of straightening out the corners, but he was doing it on the straights, too, very sure of himself and willing to go different places when they seemed good places to be instead of holding a hard line like most, who pick a groove and settle into it.

On the 150th lap, as he entered turn three, Mario got caught in the draft from Mike Mosley's car and the air currents whipped him out of control and twisted him up towards the wall as the fans screamed. "I was sleeping out there, too relaxed," Mario admitted later. "I didn't expect what happened and it startled me and the car got out of control and started to slide up into the wall. I was sure I was going to hit the wall and I just knew that was that and it really shook me, but I steered like crazy and somehow I got it back into control before I hit the wall, and straightened out and found my way again and it sort of woke me up."

Four laps later, with 115 miles to go, he darted into his pit for his last load of fuel. His crew tried to get him out a little faster this time, but as they did, Brawner slipped as Mario was accelerating, and Mario ran over his leg and knocked him aside, but kept on going. Brawner wasn't seriously hurt. He was helped up, with tire tread marks on his coveralls and a bruise on his leg, and limped the rest of the way back. Jim McGee kept flashing the E-Z sign to Mario as he rolled round and round in the lead.

Andretti eased off. Gurney was two laps back, Unser three laps. All Mario had to do was keep going at a reasonable rate, but the way cars collapse in the clutch at this place, he did not feel sure of anything. Foyt, many laps back, came up to him and acted as though he wanted to race him for fun, but Andretti let him go. "The temptation was there. It was tough as hell," he said later. "This has to be the best planned race I've ever run."

In the last laps, he was running low on fuel, but he was afraid to pit. Granatelli, who had been crushed in the last laps two years in a row, sat on a canvas chair in the front of the pits, his legs up on the wall, his face expressionless, waiting. Someone came up to him to ask him if there'd be a victory party and Andy looked at him, startled, and told him he must be crazy and to shut up about such things, and then returned to staring and counting off the last laps, which seemed as though they would never pass.

He and his brothers had tied headlights on an old car so they could drive to the Speedway the first time in the 1940's, poor, but hopeful, and now he sat with a roll of $500 bills in his pocket, which he had been presenting to people earlier in the day. He was rich, but resisting hope.

Andretti took the white flag which meant he

was going into the two hundredth and last lap. He rolled around while the crowd stood and cheered him, and after three hours and eleven minutes and forty-one seconds he took the checkered flag as he crossed the finish line. In the stands Dee Ann Andretti said, "I think I'm going to faint," and then she fell into the arms of her friend and wept. In the pits Andy Granatelli stood up and looked around as though he could not believe it, and all around him the crew was jumping up and down and yelling. He broke into a run and Brawner broke into a run and out of the stands came Dee Ann Andretti running as Andretti was driving around toward Victory Lane, almost empty of fuel now.

Fat Andy and fat Dee Ann, the one fat from good living and the other fat only from pregnancy, and gaunt Brawner, gimpy from his accident, hurried to the celebration, huffing and puffing and so excited they could hardly stand it. Granatelli got there first, before even Mario did, and as the cool little driver steered his bright red car in, Andy was waiting for him. He slapped an STP sticker on the huge Borg-Warner Victory Trophy and one on Mario's shoulder and gave him a great bear hug and kissed him on the cheek furiously, once, twice, three times, before Dee Ann or the queen could get at the smiling, greasy, weary, sore driver, who yelled, "Hey, you're a lousy kisser."

Someone shielded Dee Ann from the crush

and helped her to him. They all got into the pace car, which was theirs now, since it goes to the winner, and sat on the top of the back seat, a laurel wreath draped around Mario's neck and a bouquet of flowers in Dee Ann's hands and a great smile on Granatelli's face. Later he said, "I felt like Pancho Villa or something." Dee Ann said, "I was so proud of Mario." And Mario said, "I have never been so full of emotion in my life."

In the interview room, Dee Ann found a seat in the corner, rather than on the platform. A shy, girlish person, she said, "I used to be able to relax. When Mario was running in midget races, I used to fall asleep in the car in the infield. As I've gotten older, I've become a lot more nervous." Someone asked Brawner if he would retire now, and Brawner said, "No. I've changed my mind." And everyone laughed, and his wife, Kay, said, "It couldn't have happened to a nicer man."

Granatelli yelled, "Hey, Mario, I told you you'd never win the 500 until you drove for me." And someone asked him if he was going to retire then and Andy shook his head and said, "Of course, not. For twenty-three years I don't win and now that I win you think I'm not coming back. I'd like to win it the next twenty-two years in a row just to get even."

Mario seemed the calmest of all, very cool. His face remained severely marked by the burns. "I guess it hurts," he said, "but I was too busy to think about it until now." He talked about the race and how hard it had been to drive conservatively and how he almost lost it on the 150th lap. He had to admit he doubted they could have won if they had been pressed to greater speeds. He felt that the Lotus might have been the better car but this car had proven it was good enough and he was almost glad now the accident had happened, despite the burns. It now seemed to him that if it wasn't your year to win, something was going to go wrong, and if it was your year you were going to win no matter what went wrong. This had to be the greatest thrill of his life. And then someone asked him if he might retire and he looked startled, as though the thought had never crossed his mind. He said, "No. I'm a race-driver and I'm going to go on driving races."

10. The Modern Knight

IN ATLANTA, the night before one race, some of the drivers changed into bathing suits and were swimming in the motel pool while others were standing around in civvies cutting up. One of the swimmers shoved little Andretti, clad in a business suit, into the pool. Mario climbed out, dripping wet, and without saying a word, went inside, took off his clothes, put on the

*swimmer's business suit, went back out-
side and jumped into the pool.*

In Indianapolis, the night after the 1969
race, Mario Andretti seemed the calmest soul
around. After the last hurrah had died down at
the Motor Speedway, after the track was emp-
tied and the night closed in and the wind blew
the debris about, the victory party convened at
the trailer in which the Andrettis had tempo-
rary residence. Three bottles of champagne,
which Dee Ann Andretti had confidently placed
on ice, were popped and downed amid toasts to
the new champion. Smiling cool, Mario
shrugged. "I always knew I'd win the 500," he
said. "I just didn't know when."

He had averaged 156.867 miles per hour to
win the ancient classic which had eluded him in
five previous tries. At the Victory Banquet, he
collected the highest single race prize ever,
$205,727.06, out of the largest purse in racing
history, more than $800,000. Then he went
back to work.

Prior to Indianapolis, he had lost after leading at Phoenix, then won Hanford easily. During the Hanford race, mechanics were working
on Art Pollard's car in the pits when it burst
into flames. One of the mechanics, Red Stainton,
jumped backwards. As he did so, he went into
the path of Andretti's car, which was charging
into an adjoining pit for fuel. Mario's car

struck Stainton, who suffered head injuries and was critically hurt. Later, Andretti said, "There was nothing I could do about it. The accident naturally saddened my win. It bothered me during the race, but it's like seeing an accident on the highway. You feel sick about it, but you keep right on going to wherever you're headed."

Mario was headed for immortality, by way of Indianapolis. After his 500 triumph, he resumed the tour at Milwaukee. He took the pole with a record run. After Art Pollard in another STP car touched off a wild melee that removed ten cars on the very first lap, and then took over a second STP car, Andretti led for eighty-eight miles until his engine went sour, then gave way to Pollard. Having eliminated the rest of the opposition almost single-handedly, Pollard gave the Granatelli team its third consecutive triumph.

At Langhorne, Andretti duelled Bobby Unser for the lead much of the way until he developed a flat tire. He finished on the flat as Unser scored. At Colorado Springs, in this third try at the Pikes Peak Hill Climb, Andretti mastered it, roaring up the winding, risky road in twelve minutes and forty-four seconds to win at 58.5 miles per hour—the slowest, but wildest, win of his championship career. At Castle Rock, Colorado, in the Rocky Mountain 150, Mario led early, but lost when he developed an oil leak.

Gordon Johncock won when Foyt spun into a crash. In the Trenton 200, Mario ran low on fuel while leading near the finish, but was being pressed too closely by Wally Dallenbach to stop. He kept going and made it to the finish first as his tank ran dry.

He returned to his hometown for the Nazareth 100 in triumph. On Friday night, there was a banquet in his honor. Dolly Granatelli mother-henned Dee Ann Andretti, who seemed especially pregnant on this evening. On Saturday afternoon, there was a parade in Mario's honor. The parade lasted three hours. Bands, some imported from as far away as Philadelphia, marched and made music. There were floats and cars full of local celebrities. Ten mayors from nearby towns took part. The town population is less than 10,000. Police estimated the crowd lining the streets at more than 50,000. Many watched from porches and upstairs windows. There were flags and homemade signs which said such things as "Mario's Our Boy" and "Mario's The Greatest" and "Hometown Boy Makes Good." Mario and Dee Ann rode in an open car and waved to their neighbors.

That night, Mario's mother prepared a great batch of linguini and homemade clam sauce for a post-race feast. Mario left early to qualify for the race. Despite a flat tire, he qualified second fastest to Billy Vukovich, then cut down Vukey early in the race and sped to a dramatic victory which had the home crowd roaring. Then he went home to host his own banquet. Dee Ann left early for the hospital. Mario went along. At 2:52 A.M., Sunday, Dee Ann delivered their third child and first daughter, a four-pound, twelve-ounce infant they named Barbara Dee. Few men could match such a period. Mario fell asleep feeling he'd had a full day.

Speaking with wistful, good-natured wonder during his stay in Nazareth, Mario commented, "Many people in town said I would never amount to anything, roaring around in the various hot rods I built when I was a kid. Maybe they were right. Here I am at twenty-nine and I still don't have a steady job." Of course, he really did have a steady job, if one with an uncertain future, and back to work he went.

In the two-part Hoosier Grand Prix at Indianapolis, Dan Gurney and Peter Revson triumphed. Mario was sidelined with a loose wheel in the first heat and crashed in the second heat. In the Milwaukee 200, Andretti had to make a pit stop for fuel, falling to fourth as Al Unser, back in action, scored. On the dirt at Springfield, Andretti won as Foyt crashed and suffered minor burns. On the high banks at Dover, Delaware, Pollard won as Andretti brushed wheels with another car, spun, hit an inside wall and demolished his car in a fiery crackup, but escaped injury. His Indy burns still had not entirely healed.

In DuQuoin, Al Unser slipped by Foyt and Andretti to win by less than ten feet in one of the closest finishes in circuit history. At Brainerd, Minnesota, on the new Donnybrooke track, Johncock and Gurney divided twin heats as Mario limped in with an ailing car fourth and third. With those points he virtually clinched his third national title. In the Trenton 300, he clinched it with his seventh victory of the season, battling the Unsers, Foyt, and Dallenbach in a wild duel, holding them off on the last laps despite a flattening tire, then limping into victory lane as the tire went completely flat.

Al Unser won at Sacramento after Andretti's engine came apart. Andretti beat Unser in the first of two 100's at Seattle, but lost to him in the second heat as he spun out twice. Unser won again at Phoenix in a two-day 200 in which Al's brother Bobby and Andretti tangled in an awesome accident. Because the race was being nationally televised, it was permitted to continue as rain began to fall and the track began to get slick. Bobby slid and rammed Mario into a slide and they twirled into the outside backstretch railing. Unser's car exploded in flames as others cars spun out. Mario jumped from his car and ran to help Bobby from his. Neither was seriously hurt. The race was stopped and completed the following day.

At Riverside, in the Rex Mays 300, the seasonal finale in which he had been deprived of the national title the two previous years in wild car-jumping episodes, Mario was relaxed, the crown in his hip pocket, and he won despite two pit stops—one to replace a loose wheel, another to add fuel. He drove brilliantly to score a dramatic, rallying triumph, then revealed that on top of his other troubles, he had lost his brakes along the way and had almost crashed three times, yet kept going to victory. "It had to be a miracle to end like this," he said in the victory circle, almost awed by the wonder of it all. His belief had been reinforced: When you are meant to win, you win.

Possibly, but the great ones win the most. In 1969, Andretti won nine title races. Only one driver ever won more in a single season. In 1964, Foyt won ten. In six seasons, Andretti now had won thirty title races. Only one driver ever has won more. In fourteen seasons, Foyt had won forty-two. In 1969, Andretti won his third national crown. Only one driver, Foyt, ever won more, five. Foyt also was five years older than Andretti.

Mario had already passed most of the most respected drivers in American racing history, including Ralph DePalma, Ted Horn, Rex Mays, Parnelli Jones, and Jimmy Bryan. He still had a way to go to match the Indianapolis records of Wilbur Shaw, Lou Meyer, Mauri Rose, Rodger Ward, and Foyt. With one more victory, a fourth, Foyt would set an Indianapolis record. Clearly, as the 1960's ran out, Foyt ranked as the greatest driver in American racing history and probably in world history. But as the 1970's began, Andretti was within reach of all laurels, which, if he continued his risky run awhile, might be his with good fortune.

In 1969, he earned $365,165 in USAC competition alone, far more than any American athlete ever has won in a single season, bringing his lifetime race winnings to more than three-quarters of a million dollars. With side money, not counting investments, he may have become the wealthiest athlete in history.

His contracts were firm. If he was overshadowed by Granatelli in STP promotions and advertisements, he was not overshadowed anywhere else. When Granatelli took over as president of Studebaker's STP division in 1963, its sales were $9,000,000. By the end of the 1960's, sales were $50,000,000. And Andretti was its most spectacular racing representative. Firestone had lost two straight 500's and had only eight of thirty-three starters when Andretti put it in the victory circle in 1969. It clung to Mario as if he were indispensable. A Ford executive said, "We could not have, no company in our field could have, a better representative. He is a winner on and off the track. He is a great driver and a great person. He is a true sportsman in competition and an immaculate gentleman in public life. He always does and says the right thing."

Every time Mario stepped into a racing car, he was endorsing for a fat fee not only STP, Ford, and Firestone, but American Oil lubricants, Autolite sparkplugs, Monroe shock absorbers, Raybestos brake linings, and many others. His car carried some thirty decals. He wore a Bell helmet. When he was at the track, he wore a Dupont uniform with Firestone and STP patches. When USAC threatened to outlaw such patches, Granatelli threatened to go naked. Clearly, nothing was sacred. USAC backed down. When he left the track, Mario was wearing Botany 500 clothes. When he sat in his new $100,000 home and flipped open a magazine, he saw himself in ads. When he turned on TV, he watched himself endorsing "Johnny Lightning" model racing sets. If Chuck Barnes took twenty per cent, he found Mario Andretti a fortune. If Andy Granatelli took the spotlight, he found places for Mario to make appearances even Barnes hadn't scheduled.

Mario may have made a million dollars in the last year of the 1960's. Incredibly, he may make more some years in the 1970's. Auto-racing, already second only to horse-racing in paid spectators in this country, seemed to be coming into its own. New tracks were springing up across the country, most notably the Ontario Motor Speedway near Los Angeles, a $25,000,000 project fashioned after Indianapolis, which planned an annual Labor Day weekend 500 of Indy proportions, as well as other races, and was discussing a flat million-dollar payoff to the first driver to win three of its championship classics. For such a jackpot, it would be dangerously difficult for a winner to retire. Showcasing the sport, multi-million dollar contracts were signed to televise races live into homes throughout the summer for the first time.

Some years ago, a retiring Rodger Ward remarked to Andretti that he was coming along at just the right time. "I wish I had been born and begun racing a few years later, as you did," Rodger said. "You are entering the golden age of auto-racing."

As the 1970's began and Mario Andretti turned thirty years of age, the gold was there, if slightly tarnished. Discontented with domination by Granatelli and STP, Clint Brawner and Jim McGee decided to sever their ties with that team. Andretti elected to remain with Granatelli and STP. Thus, one of the most successful auto-racing partnerships in history ended. All concerned said they were sad and sorry and let it go at that.

Brawner, who had served as chief mechanic on more championship trail victories, fifty-two, than any other mechanic, and McGee, who had served on all of Andretti's victories, signed with the Jim Hayhoe team with Roger McCluskey as their new driver. There was some speculation that McGee, who had many offers, might leave Brawner to go on his own, but he decided to remain with him for the time being. Meanwhile, it was announced that Vince Granatelli would take over as chief mechanic for Andretti's cars. All concerned said they were confident of future success.

A most ambitious racing program was projected for Andretti's future, which included Indianapolis, Ontario, and the rest of the championship trail, though probably fewer dirt-track races, and increased activity in Grand Prix and sports-car competition, including possibly a major bid in the Canadian-American sports-car series. "It is not fair to my family, but I simply cannot stand to spend a weekend at home when there are auto races going on. If there is racing somewhere, I am restless elsewhere. If there's a race, I want to be in it," he sighed.

Pretty, sensitive Dee Ann Andretti said, "I enjoy watching a race so long as Mario is not in it. If he is, I try not to panic. . . . I used to carry rosaries, but I twisted them until I've broken them." She paused and smiled wistfully. "I still carry them," she said.

Mario said, "I'll never really know what goes on inside her, but I know how it is if somebody close to you is out there. I'd rather be out there myself. I usually tell her, 'I don't worry. Why should you?' But that's a different story. I can understand her feelings, but she knows there's nothing she could do to turn me any other way."

Not long ago, Mario Andretti said, "I want to keep driving for ten or twenty years. I figure I was put on this earth to drive race cars."

What, he was asked, would he have been if he had been born in another time, before there were cars to race?

He said, "I would have been a knight."

POSTSCRIPT

IN UNUSUAL and spectacular fashion, Mario came across the finish line the winner in the 1970 renewal of the Noon-to-Midnight Sebring classic. This one was marked by the enormously impressive debut into big-time racing of movie star Steve McQueen, who competed despite a cast on his left foot, which was broken two weeks earlier in a motorcycle race. He glued sandpaper to the bottom of the cast to get traction on the foot, which worked the clutch, and he nearly beat Andretti and everyone else.

Andretti sped a Ferrari onto the pole with a record qualifying average speed of 121.954 miles per hour. Alternating in the cockpit with Arturo Merzario of Italy, he had led for 500 miles, and led by fifty miles with only one hour to go when his car broke down. He went into the pits, and, when the team Ferrari which had been driven by Ignacio Giunti and Nino Vacarella of Italy made its last stop, the team manager shoved Andretti into the cockpit.

He sped out in fourth place with forty-five minutes remaining. Ahead of him were an Alfa Romeo driven alternately by Toine Hezemans of Holland and expatriate Masten Gregory, a Porsche driven by McQueen and Peter Revson of the U. S., and another Porsche driven by Pedro Rodriguez of Mexico and Leo Kinnvney of Finland. Driving daringly, Andretti passed the Alfa and the McQueen Porsche to take second, and when the Rodriquez Porsche had to pit with a broken wheel, Andretti took the lead with nineteen minutes remaining.

However, he began to run out of fuel and had to pit with nine minutes left. He roared into the pits, picked up some fuel and roared out in ten seconds, just ahead of the McQueen Porsche, and held them off through the last few laps to take the checkered flag by less than twenty-four seconds. It was the wildest finish of the twenty runnings of the oldest of U. S. endurance tests.

The Andretti car had covered a record 1,289 miles at a new record average speed of 107.290 miles per hour. As the laurel wreath was draped on his shoulders, the weary, but smiling Andretti admitted, "Vacarella and Giunti deserve most of the credit. I just gave them a hand. And I never thought we'd pull it off."

GLOSSARY

BACK OFF—Reduce speed.

BLOWING *or* BREAKING AN ENGINE—Any time some part fails which causes an engine to come apart, at least partly.

BOTTOMING—Making contact with the track or some part of the track with the underside of a race-car.

BREAK LOOSE—When the car loses traction and its wheels spin.

BROADSLIDING—Coming through a turn sideways so as to reach a straightaway pointed straight.

BUMPING—Aside from making contact with another car, this term applies to removing a car from a tentative starting field by way of qualifying faster. For instance, after thirty-three cars have qualified for the Indianapolis 500, the slowest cars are in danger of being bumped if any cars then qualify faster.

CHAMPIONSHIP (*or* INDY) CAR—Full-sized open-cockpit racing car.

CHARGER—An aggressive driver who holds the lead as long as he can.

DEMOLITION DERBY—An auto event in which cars are crashed into each other until only one, the winner, is left running.

DIRT CAR—A car used for dirt tracks, usually like a sprint car.

EQUIPMENT—The race car, all parts included.

GASOLINE ALLEY—The garage area at a race track.

GET OUT OF SHAPE (*or* LOSE IT)—Lose control of a car.

GROOVE—The route around a race-course one driver or many drivers take which seems to them the best one. In general terms, some may take a high groove, some a low groove. This may vary in different parts of a track. The drivers try to find a "groove" which they consider the fastest way around.

HOG (*or* PIG)—A slow or awkward race-car.

HOT DOG—A cocky or wild driver.

INVERTED START—When the fastest qualifiers start at the back of the field.

LAP—One full turn around a course.

LEADFOOT—A charger.

MISS THE SHOW—Fail to qualify for a race, depending on the pre-determined size of the starting field.

MIDGET CAR—A car about half the size of an Indy or championship car.

NURSING A CAR—"Babying" it or driving it carefully.

POLE—The inside, front row starting position, usually assigned to the fastest qualifier. In the Indianapolis 500, this is the fastest qualifier on the first of the four qualifying days.

All qualifiers on each day take precedence over those who qualify on each next day here.

Shut off—When a car moves right in front of a car which must then slow down sharply, or change direction to avoid hitting it.

Sprint car—A car about two-thirds the size of an Indy or championship car.

Spoiler—A flap attached to a car to control wind stream effects.

Stand on it (*or* Put your foot in it)—To apply full acceleration.

Stroking it—Just driving around, well below potential.

FLAGS OR LIGHTS

Green—Go.

Yellow—Slow down, drive with caution, maintain position. No passing.

Black—Come into pits for consultation with official. Something may seem wrong with your car.

Blue and orange—Slower car move over so a car may pass.

Red—Stop, the race is halted, perhaps because of accident or condition which has made track unsafe. Restart usually is in single-file order in positions held at the stop.

White—Car is starting its last lap.

Checkered—Car has finished.

MARIO ANDRETTI
(Through 1969)

Born, February 28, 1940, Montana, Italy.
Moved to Nazareth, Pa., 1959.
Married, Dee Ann, 1961. Son, Michael, born 1962.
Son, Jeffrey, 1963. Daughter, Barbara, 1969.
First race, Ancona, Italy, 1953. First USAC race,
September, 1963. First championship circuit
race, April, 1964.

CHAMPIONSHIP CIRCUIT RECORD

Year	Races	Victo-ries	2nds	Final Placing
1934	10	0	0	11th
1965	16	1	6	First
1966	15	8	1	First
1967	19	8	3	Second
1968	27	4	11	Second
1969	23	9	3	First
1970	18	1	3	Fifth

TOTAL

7 Yrs.	128	31	27	3 titles

ALL-TIME STANDINGS

Championship Victories

1. A. J. Foyt 42
2. Mario Andretti.. 31
3. Rodger Ward ... 26
   Ralph DePalma . 26

National Titles

1. A. J. Foyt....... 5

2. Mario Andretti .. 3
   Ralph DePalma .. 3
   Earl Cooper 3
   Lou Meyer 3
   Ted Horn 3
   Jimmy Bryan.... 3

CHAMPIONSHIP CIRCUIT VICTORIES

1965	Track	Distance	Course
1.	Indianapolis Raceway Park	150 miles	Paved road course.
1966			
2.	Milwaukee Fairgrounds	100 miles	Paved oval mile.
3.	Langhorne Raceway, Pa.	100 miles	Paved oval mile.
4.	Atlanta Raceway	300 miles	Paved oval 1½ miles.
5.	Indianapolis Raceway Park	150 miles	Paved road course.
6.	Milwaukee Fairgrounds	200 miles	Paved oval mile.
7.	Indianapolis Fairgrounds	100 miles	Dirt oval mile.
8.	Trenton Fairgrounds	200 miles	Paved oval mile.
9.	Phoenix Raceway	200 miles	Paved oval mile.
1967			
10.	Trenton Fairgrounds	150 miles	Paved mile oval.
11.	Indianapolis Raceway Park	150 miles	Paved road course.
12.	Langhorne Raceway, Pa.	150 miles	Paved mile oval.
13.	St. Jovite, Canada	100 miles	Paved road course.
14.	St. Jovite, Canada	100 miles	Paved road course.

15.	Milwaukee Fair-grounds	200 miles	Paved oval mile.
16.	Indiana Fairgrounds	100 miles	Dirt oval mile.
17.	Phoenix Raceway	200 miles	Paved oval mile.

1968

18.	St. Jovite, Canada	100 miles	Paved road course.
19.	St. Jovite, Canada	100 miles	Paved road course.
20.	DuQuoin, Illinois	100 miles	Dirt oval mile.
21.	Trenton Fair-grounds	200 miles	Paved oval mile.

1969

22.	Hanford, Calif.	150 miles	Paved oval mile.
23.	Indianapolis Speed-way	500 miles	Paved oval 2½ miles.
24.	Pikes Peak, Colo.	12.1 miles	Paved road course.
25.	Trenton Fairgrounds	200 miles	Paved oval mile.
26.	Nazareth, Pa.	100 miles	Dirt oval mile.
27.	Springfield Fair-grounds	100 miles	Dirt oval mile.
28.	Trenton Fairgrounds	300 miles	Paved oval mile.
29.	Seattle Raceway	100 miles	Paved road course.
30.	Riverside Raceway	300 miles	Paved road course.
31.	Rocky Mountain	150 miles	Paved road course.

OTHER MAJOR VICTORIES

1967	Daytona 500-mile	Stock-Car classic.	Paved oval 2½ miles.
1967	Sebring 12-Hour	Sports-Car classic.	Paved road course.
1970	Sebring 12-Hour	Sports-Car classic.	Paved road course. (Andretti drove last hour.)
1971	South African Grand Prix	Formula 1 classic.	Paved road course. (4th American ever to win a Grand Prix race.)

Qualifying
(*—New record.)

Year	Lap (2½ mi.)	Time (seconds)	Speed (m.p.h.)	Average	Place
1965	1.	:54.11 *	166.328 *		
	2.	:54.18	166.112		
	3.	:54.25	165.899		
	4.	:54.46	165.259	165.899 *	Fourth
1966	1.	:54.11 *	166.328 *		
	2.	:54.18	166.113		
	3.	:54.25	165.899		
	4.	:54.46	165.259	165.899 *	First
1967	1.	:53.19	169.205		
	2.	:53.25	169.014		
	3.	:53.01 *	169.779 *		
	4.	:53.59	167.942	168.982 *	First
1968	1.	:53.63	167.817		
	2.	:53.57	168.004		
	3.	:53.70	167.598		
	4.	:53.78	167.348	167.691	Fourth
1969	1.	:52.80	170.455		
	2.	:53.28	168.918		
	3.	:52.87	170.229		
	4.	:53.00	169.811	169.851	Second
1970	1.	:53.48	168.287		
	2.	:53.41	168.508		
	3.	:53.39	168.571		
	4.	:53.74	167.453	168.209	Eighth
1971	1.	:51.74	173.947		
	2.	:52.15	172.579		
	3.	:52.22	172.348		
	4.	:52.45	171.592	172.612	Ninth

RACE RECORD

Year	Qual.	Speed	Place	Finish	Earnings
1965	4	158.8	3	200 laps	$ 42,551
1966	1	165.8	18	27 laps.	$ 25,120
1967	1	168.9	30	58 laps.	$ 21,098
1968	4	167.6	33	2 laps.	$ 9,843
1969	2	169.8	1	200 laps.	$205,727
1970	8	168.2	6	199 laps.	$ 28,202
1971	9	172.6	30	11 laps.	$ 13,260

USAC EARNINGS

1964	$18,466	1967	$108,376
1965	$96,407	1968	$109,102
1966	$95,701	1969	$365,165
		1970	$100,658

Total—$883,835